D1435482

Cooking for Love

MARIA FLORIS

Cooking for Love

PUTNAM

42 GREAT RUSSELL STREET

LONDON

Made and printed in Great Britain
by W. & J. Mackay & Co. Ltd., Chatham
for the publishers Putnam & Company Ltd.

DEDICATION

Dedicated to the memory of
B. SEEBOHM ROWNTREE, C.H., J.P.,
the first Chairman of my Company
and my greatest confidant, support and friend.

CONTENTS

CONTENTS

COOKING FOR LOVE

THE REASON FOR THIS BOOK

A little while ago a publisher paid me the honour of asking me to write a cookery book. Before I began I thought, "I shall have to see what other people have done before me in this line." Once I was told by one of Somerset Maugham's friends that Maugham read ten thousand words for each one he wrote. I resolved to take his example to heart.

Since cooking is my profession, hobby, and main interest in life, I had naturally come to know the most important cookery books already. But before jumping into an adventure like this I wanted to read them all, so that I could avoid duplicating what others had already done. I had no idea how many there were. I therefore obtained and read—or at least glanced through—many cookery books published in England, France, Italy, Austria, Germany, the United States, and even French Morocco. Then I thought to myself, "All these thousands and thousands of cookery books everywhere, and where is the result of their teaching?" And then: "Why should I add another to the multitude?"

If I could have said that they were all bad, that might have been the answer; although I cannot imagine why I should have expected to succeed where everyone else had failed. But in fact, of course, they are not all bad. Some are rather poor. Many are indifferent; they don't do any harm, and they don't do any good either. Some are good—very good; so what reason could anyone have for writing another?

I should think the only good reason for writing anything is a belief that nobody has written quite the same before. Cooking, of course, is a big subject; but already I had discovered that various writers had specialised in particular branches, and different kinds of cookery had whole libraries of books to themselves. Titles have become more and more improbable with the increasing difficulty of being original in this heavily ploughed field. I thought the end had surely been reached—until I read in a news-magazine of a brand-new cookery book that is surely unique. It is *The Bible Cookery Book*, and the author, Marian Maeve O'Brien, is a Sunday School teacher. She is also Food Editor of a St. Louis newspaper—it is hardly necessary to say that this is an American addition to the world's culinary library—and she has used her Biblical knowledge to compile a book of five hundred recipes. Each is related to a Biblical menu. Appetisers in the pre-Christian era, says the author, were almost exactly as we know them today, and were an integral part of Biblical meals. In the countryside where Jesus was teaching, a housewife offered her guests a bowl of vinegar, with pieces of bread for dipping into it, while they were waiting for the table to be laid. One O'Brien appetiser, consisting of cream cheese balls rolled in chopped dried beef, is called "Burning Bush".

I knew I could not compete with that; and I doubted more than ever my right to produce yet another book on the science and art of cookery. Yet I still had the feeling that in spite of all that had been written on the subject, I might perhaps have something to add—something that had not, to my knowledge, been said before. I would not write another general cookery book, as if pretending that none had been written before; nor would I write a highly specialised book. I would write what I can only call a personal cookery book.

My first experience of food and cooking was in another land in another age. In the Hungary in which I was born and grew up, food was of great importance indeed. Almost from infancy every girl—in every social class—was taught that she must become a good housewife and a good cook.

The old saying, "The way to a man's heart is through his stomach", was not a joke to us. Hungarian men took food seriously, and if a girl did not become a good housekeeper and cook then either her marriage would be troubled or she would not get a husband at all.

My mother was a wonderful cook, but I heard all the time that she was very poor compared with my grand-mother, whose larder looked like a delicatessen shop. My father was an extremely good-humoured man with very wide interests, but his mood was greatly affected by the quality of a meal. So my mother saw to it that a bad meal should never reach the table. She supervised all the cook-ing and tasted the dishes before they were served.

This was my home background, so far as food and cook-ing are concerned. I shall tell later of what I learnt of the subject when I became a business woman, after I had grown up, married, and had two sons. That was still in Budapest. But for the last twenty-seven years I have lived and worked in England, which has the best food (if not always the best cooking) in the world. I had to adapt my cooking, and adopt native ideas. At the same time I found that some of my foreign ideas could be adapted to English kitchens and even to English palates.

While I have lived in this country I have also travelled a good deal abroad. I have been in many different lands; and, like all travellers, wherever I have been I have had to eat. I have never regarded this practice as a regrettable neces-sity, and for me every vacation is something of a bus-woman's holiday. When I come across a dish that is new to me I am never satisfied until I have tried doing it my-self. And cooking, I think, is a subject about which one should never cease to learn.

I do not mean that I go round the world armed with a pencil and notebook writing down recipes. What I collect are ideas—and they need not be the ideas of the creators of the dishes that take my fancy. For example, once in Germany I was served with a very decorative-looking veal cutlet. It was fried a nice brown, and in the middle of the meat was a round yellow patch, with a red cherry in the centre of the patch. I thought, "What a good idea! Veal with pineapple." To my disappointment when I started to eat it I found it was yellow custard surrounding the cherry. Since then I have made this dish at home—but I put a ring of pineapple on the cutlet, still with the cherry in the centre. That is what I mean by picking up ideas abroad.

Now everyone can cook, more or less, with or without a cookery book. Most people have one or more cookery books containing what might be called the standard recipes —and very good they are, too. What I want to do here is to suggest how meals can be made just a little more interesting, usually at little extra expense or work. My aim is especially to show how to achieve more variety; for to my mind variety in meals is nearly as important as the quality of the food. You can get tired of any dish, however good, if you have to eat it too often. I should like to illustrate this with a little story. I shall be interrupting the cooking hints with quite a lot of stories as I go on, so I may as well begin doing this now.

I had a great friend who eventually moved from the town where we both lived. Sometimes he had to return on business, and many of his friends invited him to lunch or dinner. Choosing the right menu was no problem for them, as it was known that he was especially fond of a particular dish. Once when he came to dine with me I departed from the routine, in the hope that I could tempt him with some other dish. When he was leaving he thanked me for my hospitality and for giving him something different to eat. He had been back in the town for a week, he said, and for lunch and dinner every day he had been given nothing except his favourite dish. "Only," he said, "it isn't my favourite any more. I never want to eat it again." Which only shows that while a hostess should remember her guests' favourite dishes she should also know how to forget.

I was talking about the importance of variety. This does not necessarily mean buying exotic new foods—I shall suggest using a few that are not always easy to obtain in this country, but if necessary alternatives can often be bought instead; nor does a change necessarily mean a complicated new recipe—often just a slight addition or substitution is enough. The housewife may be limited in her choice of foodstuffs by many factors, and she may be limited in time, but there is never any need to go on cooking the same thing in the same way.

All the senses except hearing are involved to some extent in the process of eating, and dishes should not only taste good but look good too. Presentation is important in everything, and especially in food. How we arrange and serve dishes is an important factor in the success or failure of a meal. Our digestive juices begin to work when we see a well-arranged, appetising dish, and the colour scheme is almost as important as the flavour. So for practical as well as aesthetic reasons I shall use some space for matters of this sort.

Such, then, is the modest aim of this book. As it does not pretend to be scientific I have tried not to be too arbitrary about quantities of ingredients. It is meant to be read, and therefore is not closely sub-divided like a school text-book; but for reference any dish can be found by looking it up in the index. It does not pretend to be comprehensive: many of the best and most popular recipes will not be found in the book at all, for the simple reason that I have nothing original to say about them. On the other hand I cannot swear that none of the advice in this book has ever been offered elsewhere. I have just tried not to repeat other writers. I have tried to be helpful—and, at the same time, not too solemn. One is unlikely to cook well without some pleasure in doing it. Cooking is a serious matter, but it should also be fun.

But now the soup is on the table. Please start, don't let it get cold.

CHAPTER ONE

WHAT'S WRONG WITH SOUP?

In most countries everyone eats soup at least once, often twice, a day.

We all did in Hungary. The well-to-do had it as a first course; but the peasant and the factory worker had it really as a main dish. After it they had noodles, savoury or sweet, and they felt absolutely satisfied and well fed. But a really good soup can be a meal in itself, and in France and Italy it often is.

Why not? A good soup is nourishing, filling, tasty, not costly, and easy to make. What more do you want? One thing—variety—and there is probably more variety in soups than anything else. At home we never had the same soup for eight or ten weeks. If you can make one you can make a hundred.

Yet in Britain soup is strangely neglected. I think the people are missing a lot. It is especially avoided by those who need it most—heavy manual workers.

During the war I started my works canteen. It was not the easiest time to do this, but I just could not tolerate any more the way my fellow-workers fed. I saw them eating a few slices of bread with war-time sandwich spread, day after day, and I thought, "Nobody can live on this food, and surely nobody can work on it." So I asked the Food Office for a canteen licence, and this was granted and we started our canteen. I just announced one day to my people, "From tomorrow on, you will get a lunch." The food was free, and it still is.

1

I started off with soup, meat and two vegetables. The lunch was very popular—but the soup was not. During the war my staff was nearly all English, and nearly all men—as pastry-cooks almost always are—and they just would not eat my soup. I took this as a challenge and tried all kinds of soup on them—thick and clear, fish soup, vegetable soup, everything I could make with the materials there were then. All to no avail.

Now I have a United Nations of workers (not always very united), with Poles, Germans, Italians, Austrians, Hungarians, Swiss, and French. Of course the English are still the majority—but from time to time the canteen cook has to make soup.

Perhaps I am wrong, but I have the idea that soup is just a little more popular—or a little less unpopular—now than it was then. Britons who have spent holidays abroad—and there are no greater travellers—have had soup in their diet, and perhaps in time it will even become a national habit here too. I hope so.

To make a good soup, of course, you should have a good meat or fish stock; although at a pinch some quite good soups can be made with water instead. All general cookery books contain recipes for stocks, but these do not have to be followed too rigidly—you can vary them according to the materials you have available.

Meat Stock
(Two
Recipes)

For *Meat Stock* I usually buy shin of beef, with any bones or trimmings, giblets, and a little green bacon. Some recipes may tell you to cut the meat into small pieces, but it is better not to cut them too small because you should use the meat after it has boiled. It is very good with horse-radish sauce (see page 122).

The stock is better if you put some small pieces of butter into the bottom of the stock-pot first, add the meat and other ingredients, fry for a few minutes, and then add a little water. Put the lid on, boil for ten minutes or so, and then, when the stew is nice and yellow, add the rest of the water and let it simmer slowly for hours. The more gently you cook it, the better the meat will taste.

The other ingredients might include onions, carrots, celery—celeriac, if you can get it—a few peppercorns, and a small piece of mace.

Another Good Stock can be made with two and a half II pounds of veal and beef bones and bacon rind. Brown them in the oven with slices of carrot, onion and parsnip, then add three and a half to four and a half pints of water, enough to cover all the vegetables and bones. Let the stock cook slowly for four to six hours, and add any amount of herbs you like and salt and pepper. When it is boiling skim off the fat and strain. Then add some more water and pour the whole thing back on the bones, add any other scraps of meat you have (except lamb), and let it cook very slowly for another three to four hours, until it reaches the consistency of thick brown sauce. Pour it in a screw-topped jar and keep in the refrigerator. It is a very useful ingredient for very many good dishes or soups.

If you want a very strong *Brown Stock* for sauces, add *Brown* some knuckle of veal, a few mushrooms and tomatoes, and, *Stock* of course, more seasoning.

If you want *White Stock* you have to make it from *White Stock* chicken and veal. The vegetables are the same but no mushrooms or tomatoes, of course.

A good *Jellifying Stock* is made from chicken feet. Put *Jellifying* them in hot water for a minute or two, and then the skin *Stock* comes off easily: boil for two hours, or even longer, then remove the feet. I think this makes an even better jellifying stock than calves' bones.

From the stock you can, of course, make an almost *Singer's* infinite variety of soups. There is *Singer's Soup*, for *Soup* example. For this you peel four celeriac and boil them in the stock until tender, then add two ounces of well-washed sago. While the sago and celeriac are simmering beat up one or two egg-yolks with a quarter of a pint of cream. Stir them quickly into the hot soup, and serve immediately.

Why Singer's Soup? Because if you could not sing before, you will be able to after this soup. Maybe a new career is opening for you.

Consommé   *Consommé* is, I think, the king of soups. I suppose nearly everyone knows how to make a consommé, and there are many different very good recipes. I usually begin by making a stock from light beef bones and chicken giblets, boiling them in water very slowly for at least three hours. After skimming the top to remove any fat, add minced beef and more water, simmer gently for an hour, and then add the vegetables. Tomatoes, carrots, a parsnip, a very little cabbage, a couple of sticks of celery, a celeriac, a medium sized onion, a leek—yes, and a piece of garlic—four or five peppercorns, a piece of pimento if you can get it—each has something to add to the flavour to make this a real soup king. Slice the vegetables into big pieces before putting them in. Simmer gently, then reduce the heat and add two or three beaten egg-whites with the soup just under boiling point. Bring to the boil, and cook very gently for two hours. Drain and allow to cool, remove the fat from the top. This soup can be garnished with great variety. If you know how to make a consommé you know at least thirty-six other soups.

Pearl Barley Soup   *Pearl Barley Soup* is a good garnished consommé. Boil the pearl barley in water for thirty to forty minutes, then add to the consommé. Meanwhile mix two or three beaten egg-yolks, with some creamed butter, add to the consommé, decorate with parsley—and serve.

Consommé for Kings   If consommé is the king of soups, what is *Consommé for Kings*? The same thing with an exceptionally decorative garnish. Beat four eggs really well, add salt and red pepper (paprika), mix with a quarter of a pint of hot consommé. Put in a greased fireproof bain-marie and allow to poach very slowly in the oven. Finally cut into small squares—you will know when it is cooked if the knife comes out clean—or any other shape you prefer. This garnish can be used for any clear soup, and coloured just before serving according to the table decorations—for green add spinach water, for pink tomato purée, and so on.

Consommé Julienne is famous, and rightly so. I cut the vegetables—two or three carrots, a very little cabbage, two or three lettuce leaves, kohl-rabi, celery, celeriac, and just a little onion or leek—into thin strips; put them in a stew-pan with a very little warmed butter, add one lump of sugar, cover and allow to simmer for six or seven minutes; then add water to the soup and boil slowly until the vegetables are tender. If you cannot get kohl-rabi you can use a little turnip instead—but it must be very little, or it will kill all the other flavours.

Consommé Julienne

Peasant Soup Garnish is almost the same, except that you use French beans and other available vegetables, also chopped hard-boiled egg. Mix with red pepper or red pimento for the colour. You may even use a little chopped truffle.

Peasant Soup Garnish

Invalids need soup, and for building up the sick and convalescent—and to keep healthy people happy and well —you cannot go wrong with Double Consommé, which appears on some menu cards as *Consommé Volaille*. Put two pounds of minced beef with two quarts of cold water, and boil with a little salt very slowly for three hours. Add to the soup all kinds of vegetables—but, again, be careful with the turnip, or it will overpower all the other flavours. Boil for another twenty to thirty minutes, then clarify with two or three egg-whites. Boil for another half an hour. Now take off all the scum, sieve through a cloth, and put the clean soup back into the saucepan. Meanwhile roast a boiling chicken for half an hour. Add this and all the giblets to the soup. Let it boil for an hour, take out the chicken— which can be served separately with a sauce—then sieve it again. Before serving, add a lot of chopped parsley, mixed vegetables, or very fine noodles; or any other garnish you like.

Consommé Volaille

Why not be a pioneer? If you make a clear soup, for a change put just a little saffron in it. It has a very pleasant flavour, interesting and unusual. Of course you have to be very careful with it, as with garlic flavouring—it can make a dish, but if used excessively it can spoil it.

Mushroom Soup (Clear)

A *Clear Mushroom Soup* is quite delicious and easy to make. Just chop some onions and sauté them in a little butter until golden brown, then add the mushrooms (already peeled and chopped, of course) and a little black pepper. Pour on meat stock, and add seasoning to taste. If you like you can add a handful of well-washed rice. Boil the rice 10-15 minutes before serving and thicken the soup with just a little cream or egg-yolk—and there you have a delicious, perfect soup.

Mushroom Soup (Cream)

For *Cream of Mushroom Soup* begin in the same way. Chop a Spanish onion very finely and sauté it in butter for five or six minutes. Add the peeled, chopped mushrooms, and sauté for another two or three minutes. (You should always use butter for mushrooms—they never taste so good if done in oil or lard.) Sprinkle on some flour, and go on cooking for another two minutes or so, then add meat stock (or milk or ordinary water) and bring to the boil. Add two or three tablespoons of tapioca, and let it boil in the soup until it is clear. It should look glazed. Season with salt and black pepper; grind the peppercorn freshly, that way it has a much better flavour. Before serving, add one or two egg-yolks mixed with a little fresh cream. Stir into the hot soup, but don't allow it to come to the boil again. Finally, just before putting the soup into the tureen, add a generous amount of chopped parsley.

A word of warning: whether you make a clear or thick mushroom soup, it can only be really good if you use plenty of mushrooms!

Cream of Asparagus

Of the thick vegetable soups it would be difficult to beat *Cream of Asparagus*. You need thin, green asparagus for this. Scrape it first, of course, and then boil it in salted water or chicken stock for only six to eight minutes. Take the asparagus out of the saucepan, cut off the tips, and keep them warm. Make a roux with butter and rice flour, heat it for two or three minutes, then add the water or stock in which the asparagus was cooked and also the asparagus stalks. Boil for half an hour, then pass through a sieve; bring to the boil again, and skim. Take two or three egg-yolks with a little cream and a little butter, and mix very well. Pour the hot soup on this mixture, garnish with the asparagus tips, and serve with chopped parsley.

Celeriac is very cheap when in season, and it makes an excellent soup. Take four or five celeriacs, peel, and cut in very thin slices or shred. Boil in a little salted water, and take out when cooked. Make a roux with potato or rice flour and butter, add the water the celeriac was cooked in, and boil for ten to fifteen minutes. Put back the shredded celeriac and let it boil until tender. Put two egg-yolks in a soup tureen with a little cream, stir well until blended, and pour the soup on this. Lastly drop in chopped parsley very generously. Serve with bread croûtons fried in butter or just browned in the oven and left unbuttered. *Celeriac Soup*

Minestrone, one of Italy's many gastronomic gifts to the world, is not really a soup at all. It is a meal—and so easy. Sliced vegetables—onion, carrots, leeks, tomatoes, celery, celeriac, a very little green cabbage, and, of course, potatoes—with a pimento and salt and pepper—go into the stew-pan together with a little fresh bacon. Cook slowly until the vegetables start to colour, then add stock or water and cook for a good half-hour. Then add the green peas and French beans, and some broken spaghetti or rice. Cook slowly for another thirty to thirty-five minutes— throw in a little ham with a clove of finely chopped garlic and a pinch of chives—served with grated Parmesan cheese. That's one way of doing it. *Minestrone*

Cabbage Soup—does that sound dull? Well, now—I was in Berlin once, and I was invited to a most elegant home. My hostess was extremely interesting, cultured, elegant, a little delicate. She looked like a French porcelain doll. Everything in her home was beautiful, the furniture and decorations were all in exquisite taste. Food was *Cabbage Soup* unimaginable in such surroundings—I could not believe she ate like the rest of us, I thought she lived on rose-leaves.

But lunch was announced, and to my surprise my hostess asked if I liked soup.

"I love soup," I said.

And we started the meal with—*Cabbage Soup*. Believe it or not, it was as exquisitely tasteful as everything else in that house. I am happy to pass it on.

You begin by boiling together some lean pork and bacon in water. Skim off the fat, then add vegetables—carrots, leeks, parsnips, celery—and cook gently for an hour. Prepare two medium-sized cabbages, throwing away the crude outer leaves and the core and thinly slicing what is left. Add to the soup, and boil for another three-quarters of an hour. Then add three or four potatoes, cut into small squares, and boil until these are soft. Add a breakfast cup of fresh cream. Warning: do not let the soup boil again after you have put in the cream.

Cream of Potato

Cream . . . *Cream of Potato Soup* is one of our own family favourites, and we like it either hot or chilled. It looks good if it is snow-white and garnished with lots of chopped fresh parsley—and it tastes good! It is so easy. Peel some potatoes and cut them into small squares, then boil till soft. Mix some cream with a spoonful of potato flour, and put this in as well. Bring to the boil. If you like a slightly piquant flavour, add a little vinegar and a lump of sugar. You can use yellow butter beans instead of potatoes if you like.

From potato alone you can make several kinds of soup, all very good. Celery and celeriac provide what might be called a more sophisticated soup. When you are in an extravagant mood you can make a wonderful soup from artichokes.

Cream of Artichoke

Boil the artichokes in stock. Press out all the leaves so that all the flavour comes out. Cut the cooked bottom part of the artichoke into squares and put it in the soup tureen.

Add half a pint of cream, pepper and salt to the stock, and pour it into the tureen. Before serving add chopped parsley.

Russian Bortsch is a wonderful soup, and quite easy to make. Boil one or two pounds of good gravy beef for an hour, and then grate half a pound of beetroot into the beef stock. Boil it for twenty minutes, and then whip two egg-whites to froth and mix with the beef juice and beetroot. Let it simmer for half an hour, then strain. Season with salt and pepper, and serve with sour cream which should be in a wooden bowl. Sometimes red cabbage is used instead of beetroot. Once in a Russian house in Berlin I had an entirely different Bortsch, made from spinach and chopped lettuce leaves with a very good beef stock, brandy, Madeira wine, and sour cream.

Russian Bortsch

Tomato Soup is one of the best-known of all soups, yet it is rarely perfect in restaurants. There is only one secret in making it: you must put in enough tomatoes, fresh or purée, a little butter and salt, and sugar to reduce the acidity, and cream, which improves it enormously. If you like you can mix an egg-yolk with a tablespoon of flour and a little salt, and add it to the boiling soup drop by drop. Let it boil up, and serve with chopped parsley. You can also garnish tomato soup with a handful of well-washed rice, but cook it a little in water beforehand as otherwise it would not get tender enough in the tomato.

Tomato Soup

Chopped parsley, I think, improves any dish: it makes it more refreshing. Many soups are also improved with chopped chives. Another favourite herb of mine is dill, which has a very delicate and pleasant flavour. I use it to flavour sauces, soups, and vegetables. I also use it for decoration—it is outstandingly graceful. You can buy it in a herb-shop or grow it yourself from seeds. You do not need a garden—it will grow in a window-box.

You can make soups from everything. You can make them from all the vegetables that exist—and from some that don't exist! An excellent soup can be made from weeds, a splendid vitamin-rich soup can be made from the young leaves of nettles.

Nettle Soup   I learnt *Nettle Soup* from a German friend, who also taught me how to pick nettle leaves without getting stung. You simply put your hand under instead of over the leaves. I was sorry that I did not know this trick before, because it would have made my childhood happier. I hated nettles, and they stung me everywhere . . . I was so sensitive about them that I shall never forget.

Gather a good basketful of young nettle leaves. Boil them in a very little salted water, then chop them fine or pass them through a sieve. Add a good chicken stock or water, season with salt and black pepper. Boil for ten or fifteen minutes, then add one tablespoonful of flour mixed with three or four tablespoons of cream and one egg-yolk. If you like, season with lemon-juice, and serve with small bread croûtons.

When I was about seventeen a very poor young woman used to come to our house to attend to our hair. She made her meagre living as a sort of travelling hairdresser, going from house to house dressing people's hair in the hair-styles that were fashionable at the time. She was not much older than I—about twenty-five—but was very plain, thin, and under-nourished. She came from a large family, and had many younger brothers and sisters and many old folk to look after. She used to tell my mother about her home, and mentioned that about three or four times a week

Sorrel Soup   they had *Sorrel Soup*.

"It's very healthy indeed," she would say. They picked the sorrel in the fields as one might gather mushrooms.

One day she arrived in a terrible state, with tears pouring down her thin cheeks. The lodger was giving notice— a young dentist who had stayed with them a long time and was an important source of the family income. Now he was taking a flat for himself, and she complained bitterly of his ingratitude after all she had done for him. I think the poor man was fed up with the Sorrel Soup.

In spite of this tragedy I will tell you how to make it, for I am sure it is nourishing and I think it has a very pleasant piquant flavour. Besides, you may be particularly anxious to get rid of somebody from your household.

Chop the sorrel and cook gently in a little butter. When it is soft add water, and cook again for about twenty minutes. Add two tablespoons of flour with some more butter, cook for another five minutes, and then add two beaten egg-yolks and a cup of cream. Don't let the soup boil after the cream has gone in. Garnish with toast cut into matchsticks. I like this best if it is done by putting the bread in the oven and leaving it until golden brown and very crisp.

For *Spring Soup*, cook equal parts of spinach and sorrel with some spring onions and chopped parsley. The spinach and sorrel should be finely shredded, the spring onions chopped; and they are best boiled in chicken or veal stock, although water will do. Now make a roux from equal parts of butter and flour, let it brown to a golden colour, and then add a cup of cold water. Let it boil for a few minutes, then add it to the soup. Before serving, mix some thick cream with one or two egg-yolks, and pour this into the soup. Add some freshly chopped parsley and, if you like, some cress (watercress or mustard cress). Garnish with very finely shredded French bread roasted crisply in the oven.

Spring Soup

There are many good ways of making *Onion Soup*, and one of the best I have ever had—it was in a hotel in Düsseldorf—was really a meal in itself. It was chocolate-coloured and thick with finely chopped onions, and in it was a poached egg, the yolk of which was lovely and soft. I have since made this soup at home, and, although it is a little expensive, I think it is worth it.

Onion Soup
(*Three Recipes*)

Chop 8-10 pounds of Spanish onions (reckoning about a pound per person) very finely, and sauté them in butter until chocolate-brown. Pour on this a good brown stock, bring to the boil, and simmer slowly until the onions are very tender. Skim the fat from the top of the soup. Carefully poach one egg for each person, so that only the white is firm and the yolk remains soft, and serve with the soup.

II   Now here is a *French Onion Soup*, and I always eat it when I am in France. Reckon one large onion to a person, and slice the onions very finely. Put some butter in a dish—half an ounce for each onion—heat, and fry the onion rings in it on a low flame, stirring so that they all get a golden colour. Add a good meat stock or water, and boil for thirty to thirty-five minutes. Put two or three egg-yolks in the soup tureen, and mix well. Add to the soup the juice of half a lemon or a few drops of vinegar, according to your taste, then pour the soup into the tureen, carefully stirring the yolks all the time so that it does not curdle.

III   One more onion soup (and really there are dozens). Slice four or six large onions finely, and sauté them very slowly for a few minutes in goose fat or lard. Add about one tablespoon of flour, and salt, pepper, and garlic according to your taste. Cook all this until golden-brown, add a large bunch of fresh parsley, a little thyme, and one tablespoon of wine vinegar; and then add a good chicken or veal stock or water, and cook for about an hour. This is a very light and tasty soup.

Herb Balls   Onion soup can taste better still if you make some *Herb Balls* to put in it. Mix together some breadcrumbs, one or two slices of minced bacon, some chopped parsley, chopped chives, chopped thyme, chopped shallots, a teaspoon of garlic, and one or two whole eggs. Add salt and a little powdered black pepper. Make small balls, and boil them in the soup for twelve to fifteen minutes. Serve everybody with two or three herb balls. Before serving the soup put some chopped parsley in it.

Actor's Soup   In Hungary we had a very great actor, who was a fine artist and much loved by everyone; and he, for his part, loved good food. He had a favourite restaurant and a favourite table and, in time, a favourite soup. For the chef created it specially for him and named it after him, and then he had to like it. I think you will, too.

You need a pound or so of the best beef—from the leg or shin or the part near the ox's tail. Put this, with a pound or two of beef bones and water in a large soup saucepan and boil for half an hour. Now add a cockerel, preferably a nice fat one, cut in eight or ten pieces—use all the giblets —and boil for another half-hour. Add many vegetables all cut into long pieces—carrots, parsnips, kohl-rabi, celeriac, leek, a clove of garlic, a small onion, two or three mushrooms, tomatoes, a small cauliflower, green peas, young French beans, and salt and black pepper. Boil very gently, until the meat of the bird is tender. Remove all the meat and bones from the pan. Take the meat off the bones of the bird and cut into small pieces, using the giblets, and cut the beef in the same way. Boil some very fine egg noodles in the soup for about five minutes, remove all the fat from the top of the soup, put the meat back, and sprinkle with finely chopped parsley before serving.

A *Clear Chicken Soup* can be made in much the same way. Use chicken stock, and leave out the giblets. If you want the soup very clear, clarify with one or two egg-whites after boiling. If this is not important leave it alone, but add a very little saffron, which gives it a beautiful colour and adds flavour. Do not put the meat back in the soup, but serve it separately surrounded by the vegetables together with a good dill sauce (see page 121). You can garnish the soup with very thinly cut noodles, small dumplings made from the liver of the cockerel, or julienne (finely chopped vegetables), semolina, or rice.

Chicken Soup (Clear)

For *Chicken Cream Soup* you need to cook a boiling fowl for one and a half to two hours or until the meat is tender. Meanwhile cook two ounces of rice. When the fowl is ready take off the meat. Put aside the breast, and mince the rest of the meat and mix it with the rice, making a purée. Add this to the soup, and boil for another half an hour. Pass it through a fine sieve, and boil it up again. Skim,

Chicken Soup (Cream)

and thicken with two egg-yolks and a little cream. Cut the breast of the fowl in small diced pieces, and put these in the soup with chopped parsley. Serve very hot.

Partridge was very plentiful in the season in Hungary, and we made many different kinds of dishes from it—including, of course, *Partridge Soup*.

Partridge Soup

Put some chicken fat which has been melted in advance in a saucepan and add one carrot, a small parsnip, half a celery or celeriac and some very small onions and a leek. Brown them for a few minutes with two or three partridges, then baste with chicken stock and cook it until it is tender. Remove the breast meat of the partridges and cut it in long strips or cubes. Put it in the soup tureen and keep it warm. Take the brown meat with all the bones and chop them as fine as possible. Put in a frying pan some chicken fat and some more vegetable cut into round pieces—carrots, parsnips, half a celery and fry them together for a few minutes, pour on it one or two tablespoons of flour and brown it for another few minutes. Mix the vegetables with the chopped bones and meat and pour on it 2½ pints of chicken or veal stock and boil for two hours. Then sieve, season, add one glass of white wine and pour into the soup tureen on to the rest of the patrtridge. Serve it with croutons.

Pheasant Soup

Pheasant Soup is made in the same way.

Oxtail Soup

Oxtail Soup is justly renowned, and there are many good ways of making it. The oxtail is cut into pieces and first fried until brown with diced vegetables such as carrots, onions, and celery, and seasoned with bay leaf, peppercorns, salt and pepper. Sprinkle a little flour over it, stirring continuously for a further two minutes until the flour is a little coloured; then add stock or water, put the lid on the saucepan and allow to simmer until the meat separates easily from the bones. Remove all bones and, before serving, add a wineglass of cooking sherry and three tablespoons of milk.

Fish Soup

Every country has its own *Fish Soups*—including Hungary, which has no sea-fish. On the banks of the River

Tisza there were scores of little inns that served nothing but fish, and in these you could get wonderful fish soups, fit for a king—no, even better than that: fit for a fisherman. For the fishermen were the real connoisseurs of fish.

The soup was made in a very large stew-pan, in which some very finely cut onions, carrots, and parsnips, and one or two cloves of garlic, were boiled in fish stock.

Then they put in the fish—all sorts of fresh-water fish caught in the River Tisza. They put the very small fish in whole with the vegetables and cut the bigger fish into pieces of about two and a half to three inches long and added them later. When the soup started to simmer they added salt and a good big spoonful of red paprika, and a few fresh tomatoes if in season; and then they let it simmer for ten to fifteen minutes. The smaller fish were thrown out, and only the larger slices were served. If you never liked fish before, the aroma of this soup and the happy smiling look of the sparkling-eyed fishermen quickened your appetite so that you enjoyed it like everyone else.

I was reminded of those fishermen's inns on the banks of the Tisza when I first visited Marseilles, and found similar small fish restaurants full of seafarers and fishermen. They knew how fish should be cooked, and they were the best judges in the world of their own world-famous *Bouillabaisse*. It is really a hotch-potch of different kinds of fish with some vegetables like onions and celery and, very important, a little saffron. The fish can be crayfish, mussels, lobsters, shrimps, oysters, sole, turbot, halibut, and carp. Red paprika is needed. Its home is Marseilles, and I have never had it better than there. The only thing I would not copy from the Marseilles Bouillabaisse is that they place a big piece of bread on top of the soup. I prefer my bread separately.

Bouilla-baisse

Crab Soup was a great favourite in Hungary in months without an "r"; which meant, for many people, a magnificent crab soup on the first of May. We used to make it with twenty to twenty-four very small raw crabs—for raw

Crab Soup

lobster soup, which we made in exactly the same way, we would use two or three lobsters. Whichever you use, wash and scrub them really well before you start. Now boil some beef stock with a few carraway seeds, some black pepper-corns, and some parsley. Put in this the live crabs or lobsters, and let them cook until they are red. Then take out the shellfish, crack the shells, and remove all the meat. Cut this in small pieces, put it in the soup tureen, and keep in a warm place. Make a roux from four ounces of butter and three ounces of flour, stir it until golden yellow, add to the stock, and boil slowly for about three-quarters to one hour. Add to the soup half a pint of fresh cream, and just bring to the boil. Put the soup through a sieve, and add another quarter of a pint of cream with two ounces of butter. Mix well, and add two or three egg-yolks. Mix until well blended, sieve the soup on to the meat, and serve very hot.

Lobster Bisque

Another favourite shellfish soup of mine is the well-known *Lobster Bisque*. I have to go back in my mind to when I was very young for this recipe. I was with my parents in the South of France, and the lobster bisque we had there was, as far as I can remember, the best I have ever tasted. Of course it could have been my youthful appetite that led me into thinking this!

The soup was very rich, so rich that I could not eat anything else after it—only a refreshing lemon sherbet. If you like a wonderful but very rich soup, try this; it is really worth all the trouble.

First clean and scrub two carrots, one parsnip, and some celery and celeriac, and peel and remove the pips from three tomatoes. Cut all these vegetables in small pieces, and simmer in butter for five to six minutes. Pour on them stock or water, and bring to the boil. Put in the lobsters, which should have been very thoroughly washed and scrubbed. Reckon half a lobster per head. Boil the lobsters with the vegetables for about fifteen minutes, then pour in half a glass of brandy and a glass of good white wine. Boil for another ten minutes, season with salt and paprika, and boil with the lid on for fifteen minutes more. Allow to cool. Remove the lobsters, break up the shells, and take out all the meat. Put aside the tail and the nice pieces of meat. Mince the small pieces of meat. Cook some rice—half a cup to a cupful, depending on how many you are cooking for—and when it is creamy mix it with the minced lobster-meat and a piece of butter. Mix this with the soup, and then sieve it. Let the soup boil again for another ten minutes. Cut the lobster tail and the other nice pieces of meat that you put aside into small pieces, and place these in the soup tureen. Add half a pint of cream to the soup, and pour it on the meat. If you like to have your lobster bisque red, use a very few drops of carmine. Put chopped parsley in the soup.

Both crab and lobster can be used in *Another Fish Soup* that we used to have in Hungary, although I make it differently here because there is sea-food as well as fresh-water fish. Buy about five pounds of various fish—crab, lobster, trout, eel, and halibut, anything you like—and cut it into slices about an inch thick. Put a good-sized piece of butter, about six ounces, into a large saucepan with some bacon cut into small pieces, and sauté until it is a golden colour. Add one pint of dry white wine, one bay leaf, parsley, a little thyme, and a clove of garlic pressed through the garlic presser. Bring to the boil, and let it simmer for twenty minutes. Add the slices of fish to this brew, and cook for fifteen minutes. Add some meat stock, a strong one if you have it—if not, water will do; then make a roux from butter and flour, fry it until golden brown, and add salt and pepper. Pour a glass of wine on the roux, and stir it into the soup. Lastly add a glass of brandy and light it, shaking it to make sure that all the alcohol burns out of it. Serve with diced toasted bread. We used to serve a jar of sour cream with this soup.

Do you like oysters? Personally I just cannot swallow them—but I love *Oyster Soup*. Many oyster-lovers, on the

*Another
Fish Soup*

Oyster Soup

other hand, think it is a waste to boil oysters. This piece is not for them!

Use a very rich stock made from fish-bones; allow to boil for about two hours to obtain all the goodness. Allow eighteen oysters for six people. Wash them with a wire brush, and boil for a few minutes until they are open; remove the meat, and cut in two or three pieces according to size. To the stock add the juice of a lemon and half a pint of white wine, then drop in the oysters and cook for five to eight minutes. Slice one or two bread rolls into thin strips like matchsticks, bake in the oven with a little butter until golden-brown and serve with oyster soup.

Many other good fish soups can be made, and it is a great advantage to have a fish stock or Court Bouillon (see page 29) for these.

In hot weather—and it can get hot in this country, whatever the natives say—I recommend a summer soup.

Cherry Soup   It can be extremely refreshing. *Cherry Soup* is one of the tastiest and most decorative. You need two pounds of stoned dark cherries to a pint of chicken or beef stock (or water). Simmer the fruit for fifteen minutes. Add salt and sugar to taste. Now mix a dessertspoon of rice flour with half a pint of cream, and add this to the soup. Simmer gently for a few minutes, but do not allow to boil. When cool, place in the refrigerator, and serve well chilled. Morello cherries can be used if you prefer a more piquant flavour. Alternatively you can use gooseberries, but then I suggest you add one egg-yolk to the cream.

Jellied   *Jellied Cherry Soup* is also very refreshing. For this you
Cherry Soup   need about twelve to fourteen chicken feet. Plunge into boiling water, and then remove the skin; place in a pint and a half of cold water, and boil for well over an hour. Skim and remove the chicken feet, and add two pounds of cherries to the soup. Boil for fifteen minutes—and carry on exactly as for Cherry Soup. The jelly will take about two hours to set.

Wine Soup   *Wine Soup* will buck you up if you feel under the weather. You need two pints of white wine, the juice and peel of a lemon, and a piece of cinnamon, which you boil together for three or four minutes. Beat eight egg-yolks with sugar according to taste, add quarter of a pint of sherry to them, beat again, and slowly add the hot wine. Replace on the stove and simmer gently, stirring all the time until it thickens.

Breakfast Soup is—very metaphorically—quite a different kettle of fish. This does not contain wine to buck you up. It is rather to offset the bad effects of your having bucked yourself up a bit too well with wine. It is not well known in this country, but I think it might do very well.

In Hungary a party was not a success if the guests did not stay for breakfast, and at the really successful parties two breakfasts were served.

The first usually came between two and three in the morning, after a lot of drinks had been consumed. It consisted of a soup made from sauerkraut, and after heavy drinking there is nothing better than a good sour cabbage soup for putting stomachs in order. The juice of sauerkraut is a little bit like wine—anyway, it is a fermentation. It is a very pleasant drink, and many people drink it without cooking it. For the soup use three or four pints of it, but if it is too sour dilute it with water. Boil it, and add a thickening made of lard, flour, a little paprika, and a small finely chopped onion. Then boil for fifteen minutes. Add a pound of smoked pork sausage cut into pieces, and a pound of sauerkraut, and boil for another half-hour. Add cream to taste—but, of course, no more boiling after that has gone in.

The other favourite breakfast soup was *Dry Bean Soup*, and it was served in all-night cafés and restaurants to people who had been drinking too much.

The evening before the party, take a pound of brown beans. Wash them and place in a fairly large saucepan, and add four ounces of lard, a big onion, two and a half ounces of flour, a clove of garlic, and a good spoonful of paprika

Breakfast Soup

Dry Bean Soup

and salt to taste. Mix well. Be careful not to add too much salt, because you now have to add a pound of smoked ham or smoked pork, and that is usually very salty. When all is well mixed, pour on five pints of water and cover the saucepan. Put it in a slow oven. It should simmer all through the night and the following day until next evening. It is a wonderful soup, and the flavour has been described as like fine red velvet. Those of you who have eaten fine red velvet will know what this means.

CHAPTER TWO

HORS-D'OEUVRE, VARIOUS

I HAVE often noticed in restaurants in this country—and in other countries, too—that people who look as if they go to restaurants only rarely, for special occasions like birthdays and other anniversaries, always order *Hors-d'oeuvre*. If I am right—and I freely admit I may be entirely wrong about them—then I think they order hors-d'oeuvre firstly because they do not know what else to order, secondly because they think it is rather glamorous, and thirdly because it is something they never have at home. These are all excellent reasons for ordering hors-d'oeuvre in a restaurant, but there is still no excuse for not making it at home. Nothing is easier!

Some hotels and restaurants are famous for their hors-d'oeuvre, and I have been in three where they were unforgettable. The first was the Grand Hotel in Vienna, in the nineteen-twenties. The second was the Hotel de Paris in Monte Carlo. The third was a restaurant between Bordighera and San Remo, a lovely place in every way where we dined on a big terrace overlooking the sea on a beautiful summer evening and had the best and most varied hors-d'oeuvre variés I ever had. All these three restaurants had literally hundreds of cold hors-d'oeuvre— and when you had finished these, and felt you could not eat any more, they started to serve the hot hors-d'oeuvre, and brought them endlessly.

Of course, to make all those hors-d'oeuvre at home would be difficult indeed—but you can still make a very large variety of delicious hors-d'oeuvre with no trouble at all. Not only that, but you will find that making them gives you a lot of opportunity to use up left-overs that you didn't know what to do with before. So making hors-d'oeuvre is not an extravagance but can be quite an economy; also, as you will no doubt improvise new hors-d'oeuvre to add to the existing ones, it is interesting and exciting too. There is only one important rule, and that is to taste as you go.

Many hors-d'oeuvre, cold and hot, can be made from eggs. The secret is to use different sauces, herbs, and seasoning—always tasting as you go.

Hard-Boiled Eggs A good decorative hors-d'oeuvre can be made with *Hard-Boiled Eggs* and a coloured mayonnaise. The natural colour of mayonnaise is yellow: add a little spinach, and it changes to green, while with tomato it is pink. (But if you want it purple, blue, or black I am afraid you will have to look for another adviser.)

A simple recipe capable of many variations: hard-boil an egg, mash the yolk with a little fresh cream, chopped boiled lobster, and chopped dill, and decorate when the mixture is replaced in the white.

Stuffed Eggs Countless hors-d'oeuvre can be made with *Stuffed Eggs*, simply by varying the stuffing. Hard-boil the egg, and then cut it in half lengthways—for me it is always lengthways, I don't like it the other way; then take out the yolk and mix it with ham, or anchovy, or sardines, or crisply fried chopped bacon—or lots and lots of other things—and put it back in the egg-white. An excellent stuffing can be made by mixing the egg-yolk with scrambled eggs made with fresh eggs, a little cream, and chopped chives. If you want to be really extravagant, abandon the egg-yolks entirely and just fill the egg-whites with nice large grey caviare. At the moment you are lucky, you can buy a pound of caviare for 280 shillings, so don't hesitate!

Caviare Which reminds me: in Berlin, at a Russian restaurant, I learnt the correct way to eat *Caviare*. A huge dish of caviare on ice was put on the table, and my host told me to eat it plain with a spoon, without toast or lemon, just a spoonful at a time. Delicious—but I still prefer it with toast and lemon.

But to get back to home-made hors-d'oeuvre; and after eggs—often with eggs, too—come fish. These provide numerous possibilities for hot and cold hors-d'oeuvre, again with unlimited variations of sauces and flavouring herbs.

Then there are the numerous kinds of *Tinned Fish*, which cause no worry or work and only need to be decorated nicely—or, if you like, mixed with all sorts of other things, from potato to eggs, celery or celeriac, and almost anything else.

Tinned Fish

Fish Cocktails are generally classified under the heading of hors-d'oeuvre, and there is much scope for imagination here. Not long ago I had two schoolchildren to lunch, a girl of sixteen and a boy of twelve. I thought it would be fun to make them something glamorous, so I devised a shellfish macedoine. I used three oysters, three pieces of boiled lobster, and four or six shrimps for each person, and made a sauce from unsweetened tinned milk, a little citric acid, a little sugar, and a pinch of salt; for colouring I used ketchup. I stirred the sauce until it was smooth and thick, and then put all the shellfish in. Each person got one glass, into which I put some sliced lettuce, then the shellfish with the sauce, and, on top, a slice of pineapple and chopped lettuce. It was a great success, and the boy cried out, "It is just beautiful!" with each spoonful he ate.

Fish Cocktails

A cheap hors-d'oeuvre is *Marinated Eels*, and they are easy enough to make. Buy one or two pounds of eels and cut in slices. Sprinkle with a little flour, and brown in the oven in a little butter or oil for eight to ten minutes, then take out and put in an earthenware dish or jar. Boil a wine-glass of white wine with half a glass of vinegar and sliced Spanish onions. Season with salt and powdered pepper. Add a very small pinch of brown sugar, and boil for a few minutes; take away from the fire, and mix with one or two

Marinated Eels

teaspoons of French mustard; bring to the boil and pour on the eels. Allow to cool and put in the refrigerator, and serve cold when required.

Anchovies   *Anchovies* play a great part in hors-d'oeuvre. You can use them with boiled eggs, in potato salads, and with very young boiled beetroots. The beetroots must be really young and small, and before boiling they should be cut in half. Boil them until tender, then soak in sugared vinegar for a quarter to half an hour. Take out of the vinegar, put in a dish, and on each half beetroot put half an anchovy and sprinkle with chopped hard-boiled egg.

Sardines   If you have a few *Sardines* left over—as often happens when you open a tin bigger than you need—they come in very handy for hors-d'oeuvre. First make a tomato sauce with fresh tomatoes or tinned tomato purée. If you use fresh tomatoes, boil them, pass through a sieve, and boil once again, seasoning with salt and sugar. Add a little cream and just a very few grains of pepper, and allow to cool. Put the sardines in a glass dish or on a glass platter, and pour on the tomato sauce. Decorate with slices of green pimento and hard-boiled egg-yolks which have been passed through a sieve, or with very finely chopped parsley or chopped chives.

Mussels   *Mussels* are shell fish that make an excellent hors-d'oeuvre. Buy as many pounds of good mussels as you need, and first wash them very well. They really need to be scrubbed. Cook them in white wine, then take the mussels out of the shells and cook until the wine is reduced. Make a thick mayonnaise (see page 128), and add to it a little French mustard and the reduced liquid from the mussels. Put the mussels on a platter, and pour on the sauce. Decorate with slices of tomato and cucumber, and on the top of the sauce sprinkle chopped parsley and chives.

Stuffed   *Stuffed Tomato* is a popular hors-d'oeuvre, and you can
Tomato   stuff it with endless varieties of tinned fish. One of the best for this is tunny fish. You need small, firm tomatoes—

the smallest you can find. Make a hole in the top of the tomato, and take out the inside, being careful to remove all the seeds. Season inside with a little salt and pepper and a few drops of lemon juice, then pour out the excess juice. In the meantime cream a piece of tunny fish with butter and mayonnaise. If the mayonnaise is not piquant enough, add a little lemon juice. Work well together until the mixture is creamy. Stuff the tomato with this cream, and decorate with lettuce leaves and nice fresh bunches of parsley.

You can also stuff tomatoes with boiled rice. Wash the rice very well, changing the water frequently, then boil it in a lot of salted water for eighteen to twenty minutes. Drain. Cut some mushrooms in slices, sauté with a little onion, and add to the rice. Make a little mayonnaise. Take one green pimento, clean out the inside, making sure you remove all the veins and pips, chop it, and add to the mayonnaise. Mix in a little butter, and some chopped chives, and add it all to the rice. Blend all well together, and use to stuff the tomatoes. Sprinkle with Parmesan cheese, chopped parsley, and chopped chives.

Tomato is also very good stuffed with chopped boiled celeriac. Scoop out the inside of the tomato. Boil the celeriac with lemon-juice, a little salt, and a little sugar. When tender, dice and mix with mayonnaise or cream. If you use cream, add a little English mustard. Now stuff the tomatoes, and then put them in a dish covered with lettuce leaves. Cover the tomatoes with chopped hard-boiled eggs and chopped parsley.

Tomato and Orange makes an unusual and refreshing hors-d'oeuvre. Cut large tomatoes in round slices, and season with salt and pepper. Peel the oranges—if possible get seedless ones—and cut them in round slices. Put both tomatoes and oranges in a round dish, arranging them in alternate rings. In the middle pile up freshly boiled small garden peas. Sprinkle the whole dish with chopped parsley.

Tomato and Orange

Other
Vegetables

All kinds of vegetables—from the modest carrots and potatoes to the wonderful asparagus and artichokes—can be used in hors-d'oeuvre, both cold and hot. So can fruit, which is used in salads a great deal in America and increasingly in this country too. Herbs are a great help—but they, like onion and garlic, must be used with great discretion. Again the single rule holds good—taste as you go.

Aspic

For hors-d'oeuvre, and indeed nearly all cold savoury dishes, you can have a lot of fun with *Aspic*. It is nourishing and decorative, and can be made long in advance.

I was told once by a gelatine expert that since the Indians stopped being so very religious, and many of them became Christians, it is difficult to make the really fine gelatine. In the olden times the Indians would not let anyone interfere with their cows when they died, perhaps in a field or even in the street, no matter what their age. After a while nothing was left but their bones, which lay there for years and years. The hot sun made them snow-white, which is just the thing for gelatine-making.

I would not like to guarantee the accuracy of this story, but since I heard it I make my own gelatine, which I use for aspic.

You can easily get veal bones from your butcher—and, even more easily, chicken's feet. Both are the best things for making aspic. Wash the feet and bones very well, put them in a lot of cold water, and boil very slowly for three or four hours. If you want a vegetable flavour in your gelatine, for the last half-hour of boiling add some carrots, parsley, shallots, leeks, celery, a clove of garlic, and salt and peppercorns. Finally add egg-whites to clear (one egg-white per pint of stock), stir, and simmer for another half an hour, then sieve through a cloth and leave until cold. When cold take off all the fat from the top, and sieve once more. The jelly must be absolutely clear. Put it in a jar, and you can keep it in your refrigerator for a long time.

CHAPTER THREE

THIS WONDERFUL
LAND OF FISH

HUNGARY being a Catholic country, fish played a very important part in our diet. On Fridays and other "Days of Abstinence" you would find it on every Hungarian table. We had very good fish, too—but a very limited choice. For all our fish came from the rivers and lakes. Refrigeration then was not so advanced as it is now, and if an enterprising fishmonger imported sea-fish his neighbours quickly complained of the smell! So we ate no salt-water fish, except occasionally in its smoked state.

You can imagine how I rubbed my eyes when I came to England and saw all the different kinds of fish.

In the first month I was in this country I tasted an enormous variety, many of which I had never heard of before. I am afraid there are still quite a number that I have not yet tried out. One day, not long ago, I went to my fishmonger and started to count the varieties, but I soon gave it up. If we wanted we could cook a different fish every day for two months—and the different ways of cooking fish are even more numerous. There is really no excuse for ever getting tired of fish.

Of all the wonderful fish that come from the seas around this country none, I think, can compare with the *Dover Sole*. *Dover Sole* I will dare to say it is the best fish I have ever tasted. It should increase the tourist trade if each hotel and restaurant would cook it as well as it can be done. It needs nothing but a little care.

The care should begin when you buy the fish. It must be

27

very fresh and firm. The best Dover sole, according to my taste, are the black ones. I never buy bigger than ten to twelve ounces, and I cook them whole. If you prefer them filleted, buy the larger ones—weighing a pound or more— and ask the fishmonger to fillet them for you.

Grilled Sole   There are a hundred ways of cooking sole, all of them very good; but I think it is best just plain grilled. Salt it well first, and if you like, rub in a little paprika, then put it under the grill, with a little fresh unsalted butter. Grill it on both sides until done. Serve with browned butter and a slice of lemon and new potatoes with plenty of freshly chopped parsley.

Fried Sole   On frying fish generally I shall have more to say later in this chapter. To fry Dover sole, wash and dry well, dip the fish into a plate of cold milk, slightly salted, and then sprinkle both sides with flour. This will make a light crust which becomes golden when cooked. Place the fish in plenty of hot fat or oil, and fry until it is crisp and golden-brown. Drain and sprinkle with salt. Now put a handful of clean dry parsley in the hot fat for a second, remove and drain the parsley, and then put it back in the hot fat, this time for a minute. It will then be very green and crisp. Arrange this round the sole in a long dish on a napkin, and add a slice of lemon and a few tomato slices.

Poached Sole   One good sole dish can be made hours in advance and then just popped in the oven or under the grill ten or fifteen minutes before you want to serve it. For this you want the sole filleted, and reckon two fillets per person. Unless you have some fish-stock ready, take all the bones and make a stock by boiling these in water for at least an hour or more. Season the fillets according to your taste, chop some mushrooms and onions, and fry them in butter with salt and black pepper and generously added chopped parsley. When cool, spread the mushroom mixture on each fillet and roll it up. Place the rolled-up fillets in a well-buttered fireproof dish, standing them side by side. Pour over the fish stock, and cook in the oven for

ten to fifteen minutes. Then drain off the stock, and use it
to make a white sauce with a piece of butter, a little flour,
and a little milk. Stir this sauce until smooth, then take it
off the fire and add as much Parmesan cheese as you like
and one or two well-beaten egg-yolks, stir it all well, and
pour over the fish. Season according to your taste. You
can make this dish in the morning and then, ten minutes or
so before serving in the evening, put it in the oven or under
the grill. Finally sprinkle on it a little more grated Parmesan cheese, and serve with savoury rice (see page 139).

You will often find recipes for sole with mussels, or
oysters, little button mushrooms, peeled almonds, grapes,
and all kinds of herbs. Cooked in the right way, each of
these can make an excellent dish.

Many more dishes can be made simply with poached
sole, by adding a different sauce. I shall suggest some
sauces in the chapter on that subject. Meanwhile, don't
forget that you should never let fish really boil, only
simmer.

For poaching fish most people use the so-called *Court* *Court*
Bouillon, which is a fish-and-vegetable stock, usually with *Bouillon*
wine added. To make it I first put the vegetables in water
—a carrot, a stick of celery, a piece of celeriac, some salt,
garlic, an onion or bouquet garni. Cook this very slowly
until the vegetables are tender. Pour in a pint of white
wine, then put in any kind of fish and fish bones. Simmer,
but do not boil, for about an hour. Strain into a jar which
has a lid, and put in the refrigerator.

Fish may live in water, but once they are out of the
water they cry out for wine. Cook them in wine, and after
eating them drink more wine. The reason that the
vegetables for *Court Bouillon* are cooked first in water is
simply that the wine would not cook them tender. It is
important that the wine should already be there when the
fish goes in.

Wine is used in the dugleré, another good way of *Sole*
cooking sole. Finely chop two or three shallots, and put *Dugleré*

them in a buttered stew-pan. Add about a pound of very
nice ripe tomatoes that have been peeled and cut into
pieces. Then place the fish in fillets or slices on top. Add a
little white wine, a little lemon juice, and a little chopped
parsley. Pour in a little fish stock and salt slightly, then
let it simmer for about twenty minutes. Drain off the
liquid, and with butter and flour make a roux. Add the
liquid to it and bring to the boil. Mix an egg-yolk with a
quarter of a pint of cream, and add to the sauce. Simmer
for five minutes. Pour it over the fish and sprinkle with
chopped parsley. Serve very hot with boiled potatoes or
boiled rice.

The dugleré is also a good way of cooking turbot,
another of my favourite fish.

Sole or
Turbot
Dugleré

Butter a fish dish and sprinkle with one or two finely
chopped shallots and chopped peeled tomatoes. Lay the
fish on the top and add white wine and fish stock over it,
add salt and chopped parsley. Cover with buttered paper
and a lid and cook. Reduce the stock and thicken with
beurre manié (fresh butter and a little flour). Work together and finish off with fresh cream, lemon juice and
more chopped parsley sprinkled on top.

Fish
Soufflé

I like turbot, too, for making a *Fish Soufflé*. For this
melt an ounce of butter, add an ounce of flour and a little
milk, and cook until a smooth sauce is obtained. Remove
from the heat, stir in three egg-yolks, and the flaked
cooked fish, and season well. Fold in four stiffly beaten
egg-whites and a teaspoon of chopped chives and bake for
thirty minutes in a soufflé dish.

Cod can be used instead of turbot, but should be
seasoned more.

Oven-cooked
Cod or
Haddock

Cod is not my favourite fish, but I had a cod dish in a
Swedish house that was really good. Since then I have
made it at home, but sometimes I use haddock instead of
cod. Buy some fillets, and place them in a well-buttered
baking dish. Pour on a little lemon juice and dot with
butter, cover and put in a hot oven for eight to ten

minutes. Make a roux from butter and flour, stir until well blended, then add to it fish stock, milk, or water, stirring all the time, and let it simmer for about eight to ten minutes. Add salt and cream. Remove from the heat, and add two or three egg-yolks and a little fresh butter. Work until smooth. Season with salt and pepper according to your taste. Add some shrimps or scampi if you like. Pour this sauce on the cod or haddock, sprinkle the fish with grated Parmesan cheese and garnish with Duchesse potatoes (potato purée enriched with beaten egg-yolk) piped round the dish. Heat under the grill or in a very hot oven until it is nice and brown.

The really famous English fish delicacy is, of course, the traditional *Fried Fish*, and it would be impertinent of me to try to tell you how to make it. I read somewhere long ago that Queen Elizabeth I loved her fried-fish dinners, and insisted on a vast variety at a single meal—salmon, carp, sturgeon, haddock, pike, whiting, and I don't know how many more. I have no doubt that the English had been eating this lovely dish long before then, and in my opinion it is still difficult to beat.

Fried Fish

I am sometimes asked which of the various ways of preparing fish for frying I prefer. Generally I either dust the fish with flour by shaking it in a paper bag containing a couple of tablespoons of flour and an adequate amount of salt, or I dip it in batter or in egg and bread crumbs; but I do not think it matters much which you do. In some countries the fish are rolled in cornflour—and again the difference seems to me unimportant. What counts, in my opinion, is the frying fat.

Recently I was on the island of Ischia, which has a great variety of fish. One part of the island is in the Mediterranean and one part in the Adriatic, where the fish are small and sweet. The Ischians, I was told, liked to fry their fish in oil that was at least three years old. When I tasted their fried fish I could believe it, for I found it quite uneatable. But then I have had similar experiences in

Venice and other places in Italy. The Italians generally seem to like to let their frying oil mature, and the smell alone is most unpleasant, but perhaps only to me.

I think olive oil has too strong a flavour for frying fish, and I prefer one of the blended fats or pure lard. A very good vegetable oil that does not have a pronounced flavour is pleasant. Apart from the kind of fat you use, I think much depends on its freshness and temperature. Used fat can spoil the taste of any dish. The best heat depends on how the fish is prepared: if you use batter, the oil or fat should be very hot when you dip the fish in, almost as hot as if you were deep-frying; if you have only dusted the fish with flour you do not need the fat so hot. It is, of course, vital not to overcook the fish.

Other countries also fry fish and even have their own specialities in this branch of cooking. The French, for example, have tiny fish from the Seine and Marne called *goujons* (gudgeons), which are fried and eaten whole— each fish is no more than a bite. But there is nothing to beat the English frying fish—cod, haddock, whiting, plaice, flounder, and the rest.

Plaice   *Plaice* has a reputation as a dull fish. I think this is quite undeserved. I like it, and find it very suitable for almost any kind of fish dish. It is light and flaky, and delightful when filleted, with a creamy potato purée and a suitable sauce—dill sauce, or a good creamy mushroom sauce, for example; or with white wine and celery; or, if asparagus is in season, with asparagus sauce (see page 118). For this I first poach the filleted plaice with the bones and then, when the sauce is made, stir in one or two egg-yolks.

Once I had guests to dinner, and gave them plaice. I bought it filleted, as usual, but took the bones and boiled these for five or six minutes. I then cooked the plaice in the liquid. Meanwhile I boiled about a pound of fresh young sorrel leaves, then drained them and put them in a buttered fireproof dish. On these I put the cooked plaice, then fried some breadcrumbs in butter and sprinkled these on the fish. I served it with new potatoes, and the much-maligned plaice went down very well.

A very nice dish can be made by stuffing plaice fillets with hard-boiled eggs and anchovies and butter, all worked together. Spread the stuffing on each fillet, and roll it up. Put the stuffed and rolled fillets in a buttered fireproof dish, standing up next to each other, with a little dot of butter and cream on each, and sprinkle with Parmesan cheese. Put in the oven for half an hour.

Stuffed Plaice

Mackerel are easy to stuff if you open them down the back. Remove the bones, wash, and leave to dry; then sprinkle with salt and paprika. The stuffing can be made from well-creamed butter, chopped parsley, chopped chives, chopped fried onions and chopped fried mushrooms. Add a beaten egg, and mix well. Fill the mackerel with the stuffing. Put each fish in a piece of buttered grease-proof paper, fold it, and twist the ends of the paper two or three times. Place the fish in a baking-tin and cover. Cook in a moderately hot oven for ten to fifteen minutes, serve on a hot dish in their paper wrapping, with new potatoes which should have a lot of freshly chopped parsley on them. You can do the same thing with herring or trout. Instead of mushrooms you can use chopped ham or boiled rice.

Stuffed Mackerel, Herring, or Trout

When I first came to London somebody told us we ought to see the Caledonian Market. We went and found it most interesting, and bought a lot of things for very little money. But what amazed us was not only all the old pieces of furniture and so-called antiques, china and silver —if you were lucky you could pick up a bargain—but also the variety of food that was on sale there. I saw a fish that I had never seen before—the *Grey Mullet*; and whenever I see it now I always think of the old Caledonian Market, where I noticed it for the first time. I remember that I asked the fishmonger how to cook it, and he told me; and then I chose a few good-sized fish, and when he told me the price it worked out at a penny each. Even in

Grey Mullet

those days to buy a whole fish for a penny was remarkable
—with the recipe for cooking it thrown in free, it was
unbelievable.

We just baked it whole with seasoning and butter, and
we liked it very much—so much that I am afraid we rather
overdid it. We ate it so often that we got tired of it, and
now for many years I have not touched it. But I am still
very fond of another mullet—the rouget, or red mullet.
This fish has to be absolutely fresh. Freshness of fish is
always important, of course—so many kinds of meat and
game are improved by keeping, but I do not know of any
fish that is not at its best when absolutely fresh; and unless
red mullet is fresh it is really not worth buying.

Red Mullet   *Red Mullet* is good both hot and cold. One of my
(Hot)   favourite ways of cooking it is the simplest—seasoned with
salt and red pepper and baked in the oven in butter for
fifteen to eighteen minutes, until it is nicely crisp. When I
want it cold I bake it in butter for only eight to ten
minutes, then cool it, take it out of the fat, and put it in a
well-seasoned tomato sauce. The best way to make this
sauce is to take tinned tomato purée, dilute it with water,
add salt and sugar and some cream. The dish is chilled in
the refrigerator and served cold with a salad.

Red Mullet   Alternatively cold *Red Mullet* can be covered in white
(Cold)   wine. First clean the fish, sprinkle a little flour on it, and
then fry on each side in batter or oil for one minute only;
put in a baking tin with a glass of white wine, season with
salt and pepper and, if you care for it, add a soupçon of
garlic and very little saffron. Put in the oven for five to
eight minutes. Place the fish in a jar or earthenware dish,
and pour over it the liquid in which it was cooked. Again
put it in the refrigerator and serve cold whenever you
need it.

Red Mullet   One day on my way home I was thinking of what meals
(Wine   we should have at the week-end, and I had a sudden
Shado)   ambition to make a new dish with red mullet. We had no
guests, so I had only my husband to please; but he is not

easily pleased, especially when it is a matter of something new competing with one of his old favourites. I knew it would have to look tempting and taste good to satisfy him. In the end I decided to do it with a wine shado, which is a sweet wine sauce that I use for several sweet dishes. My husband liked this, so I hoped he would like it with the fish.

I made the sauce by heating half a pint of good dry white wine with a little lemon juice and a little sugar. Then I put four egg-yolks with just a very little butter in a double saucepan and heat that, stirring vigorously, and slowly added the wine. I cooked the sauce until it had the right thickness, stirring all the time to keep it light and fluffy. Before I started to make the sauce I had to peel and stone half a pound of grapes and put them in a sauce-bowl, which I kept in a warm place until the sauce was ready to be poured on the grapes. I had baked the red mullet with the usual seasoning in butter, but only for twelve minutes. The dish certainly looked decorative—on each plate one nice crisp red mullet surrounded by the yellow sauce with the green grapes—and my husband approved.

To bring home sea-fish recipes from abroad is like bringing coals to Newcastle, and in any case often it is impossible to obtain the right species of fish. So there is no point in describing grilled octopus, which is much loved by the Mediterranean people—not that I like it myself, and I don't think you would either—or the swordfish served at Tangier, cooked in a lot of vegetables and served with Hollandaise sauce, which I found delicious. But we can still learn some fish dishes from other nations, as they can surely learn from us.

In Italy, for example, I had a good *Turbot* dish. A slice of turbot was browned in butter, and then put in a small fireproof dish with more butter and quite a bit of garlic, which was squeezed through a garlic presser. Freshly chopped parsley and other herbs were added, and a good vegetable stock was poured on it; then it was cooked for

Turbot
(*Italian*)

about sixteen to eighteen minutes. It was served with a very tasty savoury rice, half a tomato being placed on the fish.

Halibut
(American)
In America I ate a very good *Halibut* dish. To make this, first put half a carrot, chopped, and a quarter of a small onion in salt water, and simmer slowly. Wash and dry the fish, which you shall buy sliced, and then put it in the boiling vegetable stock for ten minutes; simmer over a medium heat. Meanwhile make the sauce. Melt but do not brown two and a half ounces of butter, add flour to thicken and one-eighth of a pint of milk, and add a few drops of lemon, black pepper and salt to taste, and three or four tablespoons of the stock in which the fish was boiled. Mix well, add an egg-yolk, then pour the sauce over the fish. You can use the chopped carrot and onion for decoration.

Matelote
au Vin
Blanc
The French have a very good stewed fish dish called *Matelote au Vin Blanc*. You should have four different kinds of fish—carp, turbot, pike, and eels, or any others you like—which you cut into pieces and brown in butter in a stew-pan. Add chopped shallots, and two whole cloves of garlic, which you throw out after cooking. Finally add chopped carrot and chopped parsley, a few peppercorns, some small mushrooms, and a few small onions, and cover with dry white wine. Add a bay leaf, a little thyme, and a little pepper. Cover the pan and let it simmer slowly until cooked, then take out the fish and put it in an earthenware dish near the fire so that it will keep warm. Reduce the liquid by more cooking, drain it and thicken it with a little butter and flour. Pour this over the fish, and before serving pour on it some French cognac. Flame it before serving.

A South
African
Recipe
My younger son brought home a recipe from South Africa that I make quite often—mostly to please him, but perhaps you will like it too. Chop one onion and fry in oil in quite a large heavy saucepan, add some black pepper, salt, and garlic (if you like garlic), and fry until golden brown. Stir and add just enough water to cover, bring to the boil very slowly, and then put in several small kinds of

fish. Any fish will do. Simmer for ten or twelve minutes. Pour the liquid in a soup tureen, and serve with crisp squares of toast if you like. Sprinkle the fish and soup with lemon juice. Serve the fish in a separate dish.

The herring is one of the best-flavoured fish, and I am afraid it is less popular than it should be for the very bad reason that it is too cheap. One of the cheapest—and tastiest—fish dishes I know is *Herring Pudding*. For this *Herring* you want the herrings boned. Cut them in even slices. Peel *Pudding* and cut potatoes in even slices; then slice one or two large Spanish onions very finely and mix butter with bread-crumbs. Into a baking dish put alternate layers of potatoes, onions, breadcrumbs, and herrings. Sprinkle each layer with butter and salt, and finish with a layer of potatoes on top. Beat two or three eggs with a little milk or cream, and pour this over the dish. Then bake in a hot oven for three-quarters of an hour or until the potatoes are tender.

Pickled Herring is very useful to have for hors-d'oeuvre *Pickled* in case of unexpected guests. Clean and bone six or eight *Herring* herrings, salt well, and put them in a baking tin with a little pepper. Place in a good warm oven for five to seven minutes. Take a long dish, put in the herrings, then a lot of Spanish onions cut very finely; pour on this vinegar slightly diluted with water and season with salt and sugar —the best is brown sugar—and a few black peppercorns and some small red pimento. Keep in a cold place for three or four days. When ready, you can keep the pickled her-rings in the refrigerator for two or three weeks in a well-covered dish or jar. Be careful not to make the refrigerator smell of herring and onions.

In Sweden, which is by no means a poor country, the herring is eaten in all sorts of delightful ways. One of my favourite fish dishes is *Swedish Pickled Herring*. *Pickled*

Buy six boned herrings, but ask the fishmonger to give *Herring* you the bones separately. Boil these in water for a good *(Swedish)* half-hour or more. Clean the herrings, remove the heads. Butter a dish, and place the herrings in it with a little salt and some of the water in which the bones were boiled. Cook in the oven for five minutes. Mix half a pint of vinegar with the rest of the herring-bone stock and the liquid in which the herrings were cooked. Add two table-spoons of brown sugar, two bay leaves, a small piece of dry ginger, a very little mustard seed, a piece of horse-radish, and one sliced carrot. Slice two large red onions—finely—if you can get them—if not, ordinary onions will do. Boil all these together for eight or ten minutes. When cold, pour over the herrings, which in the meantime should have been put in a glass or earthenware jar. You can keep these herrings for weeks in a cool larder, and they are always a good stand-by for unexpected guests.

Herring Hors-d'oeuvre (Swedish) — Here is another Swedish herring recipe. Wash the herrings and cut off their heads. Soak overnight in cold water, and drain. Cut the herrings in small pieces. Boil potatoes, then fry with a little butter, and cut in squares. Add these to the herrings, together with beetroot, one apple, one large finely sliced onion, one pickled gherkin, one boiled and sliced celeriac, and one celery heart. Mix all these together. Dilute a quarter of a pint of vinegar with water, according to taste, add two tablespoons of brown sugar and black pepper to taste, and pour over the herrings. Pile up nicely in a glass dish, and decorate with tomato and gherkin, hard-boiled eggs and fresh parsley. It makes a very decorative hors-d'oeuvre.

So far I have been talking about sea-fish, of which this country has such a wonderful variety. When it comes to fresh-water fish I can draw on my own native experience—and I must confess to some nostalgic yearnings. From Lake Balaton, Hungary's largest lake, came two of the best fish in Europe—perhaps even the best in the world. These were the famous fogash and schullo. Crisp brown on the outside, flaky snow-white inside when broiled, they had practically no bones, no fish smell whatever, and a unique flavour. We cooked and dressed it as we do salmon here.

Another of our best fishes was kechege, which we

mostly did in jelly, although it was very good stuffed as well. Then there was sturgeon, plain boiled and usually served cold with a green sauce. But it would be pointless for me to give recipes for these fish when they cannot be obtained here. In any case, this country also has fresh-water fish. It is one of the few countries in the world that has a rival to the Balaton fogash—and that, of course, is *Salmon*. Apart from the difference in colour and the flakiness of the fogash the two have much in common, and for preference I cook them both in the same way.

Salmon

I am not really a friend of so-called "plain cooking", but I think it is a pity to try to do anything with salmon. I do not think you can improve on it with a lot of mixed flavours. According to my taste it is enough if you vary the sauce and salad, and leave the salmon alone. It has such wonderful flavour. So just cook it in vegetable water, and serve cold with sauce. If you want to have only one slice of salmon, about an inch thick, simmer it in a good court bouillon (see page 29), let it cool, and cover with thick mayonnaise. Put the slice of salmon on a dish, and garnish with all kinds of fresh vegetables—carrots, peas, cucumber, tomato, and half a hard-boiled egg.

After salmon comes *Trout*, a lovely fish that was plentiful in Hungary also, and very cheap. People just went out to the rivers and rivulets with a primitive home-made rod, and came back in no time with quite a lot of trout for their breakfast or dinner. In my childhood we often went out for trout picnics. First we caught the trout—and we never failed, so it must have been easy—and then we wrapped each fish in a newspaper and put it in a big glowing fire. When the paper was burnt the trout was cooked—and the skin came off with the paper. We used to eat two or three each, and I think that was the best trout I ever tasted.

Trout

Sometimes we *Baked Trout* at home, first seasoning them with salt and a little paprika and then putting them with fresh butter in a fireproof dish and baking in the oven

Baked Trout

for ten minutes. Or we grill them, or boil them and serve with several kinds of sauce.

Blue Trout   *Blue Trout* is, of course, the classic way—but the fish must be fresh, as if it had just come out of the river. Open it and wash it, but don't rub off the slimy wetness or it will not get blue. Leave it in cold water until you are ready to cook it. For each trout boil half an onion, some carrots, celery, a few black peppercorns, and fresh parsley in half a pint of water for fifteen minutes. Season with salt, put in the trout, and turn the heat right down. The trout will immediately turn blue. Let it simmer—it must not boil at all. Strain off the liquid, and serve the trout with hot melted butter, lemon, and new potatoes and chopped parsley.

Trout with   Wine was cheap in Hungary, so we also prepared trout
Red Wine   with a dry red wine. First we made a very pale roux with a little butter and flour, and then we poured the red wine on it and cooked till it was smooth but not too thick. Into this sauce we put mushrooms cut in small pieces, salt, and black pepper. Then we put in the trout, and let them simmer for ten minutes. Finally we placed the trout in a dish, strained the liquid on to it, and then put the mushrooms on the fish. Served with boiled potatoes it was delicious.

Sometimes we used the famous Tokay wine. We did it much the same way, without the mushroom but with a bay leaf and sometimes a clove. The wine had to cover the fish. It was good served with plain noodles mixed only with melted butter.

Trout with   One of the best ways of cooking the lovely English
Horseradish   trout is, I think, with a horseradish cream sauce. Clean the
Sauce   trout and arrange it in a baking dish with salt and a little black pepper, pour on just a little water, and cook in the oven for twelve to fourteen minutes. Drain off the liquid into a saucepan. In another saucepan make a small roux with butter and flour. Stir it for a few minutes, and add salt and a little sugar. Pour on it a little of the fish water, and

add quite a good portion of freshly grated horseradish. (When you grate the horseradish salt it immediately, otherwise it loses its white colour.) Simmer for a few minutes, but do not boil; add some thick cream, mix well, and pour over the trout. When serving, sprinkle with chopped parsley and chopped red pimento.

Another fresh-water fish of which we ate a great deal in Hungary is *Carp*. I might almost say it was a national fish dish of ours, but in fact I had the best carp of my life in Berlin. It was in the very famous Restaurant Peltzer, where long before the First World War a lunch cost two or three pounds per person. I knew Mr. Peltzer, the proprietor, and when I lunched there he recommended me to eat his Carp Blau. It was only cooked in vegetable water for twenty minutes, but the flavour was exquisite. For this very simple way of cooking you must, of course, have the very best quality of food. Mr. Peltzer bought his from the huge Berlin market, the biggest I ever saw. He took me round, and everyone on the stalls seemed to know him and was pleased to see him. He did not talk a lot, but just pointed his finger and said, "Send me two of these baskets of vegetable" or whatever it was he wanted. He never asked a question about the price. I was surprised, but he told me, "They know me well. They only have to sell me something that is not right in quality and price, and they will never see me any more."

You can buy very good carp in England, but you will be lucky if you don't have to finish the cleaning yourself. The first time I bought carp in this country, only a few months after I arrived, I asked the fishmonger to clean it for me properly, and he said he would; but when I looked at it at home I found it was not cleaned at all. I still have the same sort of trouble after twenty-six years. My very good and extremely obliging fishmonger always sends me carp which has not been properly cleaned. Last Christmas Eve —it is a custom in Hungary to have carp for dinner on Christmas Eve, and we still keep this up—I said to my

Carp

favourite assistant at the fishmonger's, "Charles, you have not cleaned my Christmas carp. I shall have a lot of work with it when I get home." My nice Charlie with a very innocent face said, "Oh, I have cleaned it, madam." "No, you haven't, Charlie," I said. "You have left all the scales on it." "Oh," he said, "I didn't know you wanted those taken off too." Charlie knows very well how to handle lobster, sole, salmon, and nearly every other fish—except carp. And if the fishmonger does not remove all the "money", as we call the little bits, they are very unpleasant to eat.

Baked Carp   The first time I cooked carp for English guests I baked it with butter, a lot of cream, sliced tomato, sliced onions, pimento, and a few slices of potato. Before adding it to the vegetables I seasoned it inside and outside with salt and paprika. I baked it for about twenty-five to thirty minutes, basting from time to time with thick cream. This dish looked extremely good, and when it was served one of my guests looked delighted. Rather surprised, I concluded that she had had it before. Yes, she told me, she knew it and loved it. Then she helped herself from the fish dish and, to my astonishment, took the head. She ate it carefully and gracefully, obviously with experience, and then showed me two small bones which she fished out from the head. They were little round flat bones like small coins, a little bigger than farthings. Each year, she told me, when she ate carp for the first time she always took those two bones from the fish's head, and put them in her purse. So long as she carried them with her, she had been told, she would never be out of money. "I have done this for many years," she said, "and I am much better off than I used to be before." Try it, and I hope it will help you too.

A Sauce or Jelly for Carp (Two Recipes)   This dish can be varied in all sorts of ways. When you buy carp you may be able to buy a spare head as well. At the same time, when you ask the fishmonger to clean the fish and remove all the inside, ask him to give you back the milk or roe. Now make your vegetable stock by boiling sliced onions, carrots, parsnip, celeriac, tomatoes, celery, garlic, bay leaf, and salt, together with the spare carp's head. Wash the carp and cut it into six or eight pieces, and put it in the liquid and boil up. When it is boiling put in a teaspoonful of paprika, lower the flame and simmer for ten to fifteen minutes. If you want it hot, put in a quarter of a pint of cream. If you want it jellied, take out the fish slices very carefully and put them into a long fish dish. If you can, put them together so that they look like the whole fish. Reduce the liquid and strain the juice on the fish. Decorate the fish with the carrots and parsnips, put the dish in the refrigerator for three or four hours, and serve cold.

The juice of one lemon, one stick of celery, one celeriac, *II* one onion, four or five black peppercorns, a small piece of dry ginger, and two glasses of white or red wine: boil them all together, and prepare the carp. Remove the bits the fishmonger missed, wash and slice, and put into the vegetable liquid. Simmer very slowly for thirty minutes. Take the fish out carefully, as it breaks easily. Put it on a dish and keep it warm. Strain the liquid and put it back on the fire, two ounces of butter, a teaspoon of sugar— preferably brown—a few sultanas, and a few blanched almonds or walnuts or both; and boil. Finally add one wineglass of cream. Pour all the sauce over the carp, and serve very hot.

Shell-fish are in a class of their own, and mostly people *Lobsters* either like them very much or not at all. Those who are fond of *Lobster* usually do not mind going to some trouble to cook it in just the right way. Once I was invited to a French house where the host insisted on cooking the lobster himself. We were all invited to watch. Of course, as it should be, he had the lobsters alive when he put them in boiling water. He also had a special instrument, a kind of fork, which he heated in a fire until glowing hot; and with this he fished out the lobsters and cut each one quickly in two. Then he broke the claws and served them

immediately on everybody's plate. According to him it
was very important to have the fork very hot because the
lobster would get a shock if it was fished out with a cold
fork and would lose its sweetness.

I myself would never buy lobsters other than alive, but
I have not gone to the extent of using a special hot fork
to lift them out. I just drop them in salted water, cover, and
boil according to their weight—perhaps twenty to twenty-
five minutes, but only fifteen minutes if they are small. I
let them cool in the water, then split the lobster and crack
the claws. If I want it cold I clean all the dark parts out
and arrange in a silver dish with lettuce leaves and lemon

Hot Lobster slices, and serve with Hollandaise sauce. For *Hot Lobster*
(Two I take out all the meat from the body and cracked claws,
Recipes) cut it into small slices, and arrange back in the shells, and
then put it in a fireproof dish. On this I pour a good
Parmesan cheese sauce, with a dice of butter, and then I
grill it until golden-brown. I reckon half a lobster per
person.

II *Another Good Hot Lobster Dish* can be made by cooking
it in wine. First boil the lobster, preferably in a good
strong fish bouillon or stock. When cooked, take it out
and remove all the meat from the shell, claws, and everywhere else. Cut the meat into slices—not too small—and
put them in a saucepan with salt and a quarter of a pound
of fresh butter. Stir for a minute or two, and add a glass of
good white wine and a glass of Madeira. Let it simmer for
a few minutes, then add a quarter of a pint of fresh thick
cream. Before serving, beat two egg-yolks with a little
more cream, and pour this on the lobster. Sprinkle with
freshly chopped dill, and serve with boiled rice.

Lobster or Many good dishes can be made with either lobster or
Crab Butter crab if you first make the so-called *Lobster* or *Crab Butter*.
It is very easy to make, and can be kept handy in the
refrigerator.

First clean the lobster or crab, scrubbing thoroughly to
remove all sand and mud. Then boil in the usual way, in

salted vegetable stock. When cooked, break up the lobster
or crab and take out all the meat which you can use in any
way you like. Now take the shell, dry it in the oven for a
few minutes, then put it on a mortar and beat it until it is
a nice fine powder. Fry this in fresh butter for four or five
minutes, then add a small spoonful of paprika. Stir, add
water, and boil for a few minutes. Take it off the fire and
let it cool. When cold, take off the fat from the top and
pass the rest through a sieve. Put it in a screw-top glass
jar and keep it in the refrigerator.

Lobster Mousse

Scrub and wash one or two lobsters and boil them in
vegetable water: carrots, celery, parsley, one bay leaf, one
leek, a few caraway seeds, salt and a few peppercorns.
Boil the lobster for 15-25 minutes according to size. When
ready take out of the pot, let it cool. Take out all the
vegetables when tender and reduce the water to half a pint.
Break up the lobster, take out all the meat and put aside
the nicest pieces. Mince or chop the rest of the lobster-meat
and mix with the vegetable water in which the lobster
boiled, add salt, paprika and a small piece of lobster butter,
some fish or chicken aspic warmed up and a half or one pint
of whipped cream according to the quantity of lobster
mousse you need. Mix well and taste for seasoning. Take
a round mousse mould, place in the bottom first a few
tomatoes cut in quarters and a few boiled green peas, then
pour on it a very little lukewarm aspic. Let it set in the
refrigerator for about half an hour, then pour on it the
whole mixture of the mousse. Let it set in the refrigerator
for two hours. Then take a round dish, put on it crisp green
lettuce leaves and turn out the mousse. Cut the pieces of
lobster which you put aside into thin slices, put them
round the mousse and decorate the dish with sliced
tomatoes, sliced cucumber and hard boiled eggs. Place the
lobster head on top of the mousse. Serve with mayonnaise
or hollandaise sauce.

Crabs

When in season—that is, in the spring—the small
Crabs were so plentiful in Hungary that we had them very

often. We made crab goulash, crab soup, a good crab ragout, crab with mayonnaise, and many other crab dishes. I personally liked crab best in a very simple way, just boiled in vegetable stock and served in the shell. It was a very messy business breaking it up to eat it, but this way it has a fine flavour and it is great fun to let yourself go for an hour, so that afterwards you have to wash not only your hands but even your face.

Crab Goulash   We made the *Crab Goulash* like any other goulash. We boiled the crab in vegetable water, and then took out the meat. Meanwhile we fried chopped onions in butter, and put the crab meat in this, adding paprika and salt. We fried it for five or six minutes, finally adding a few tablespoons of water and quite a bit of fresh cream and let it simmer a few minutes.

Crab Ragout   For *Crab Ragout*, boil the crab in the same way as for the goulash, and take out the meat. Meanwhile take some home-made crab butter and mix it with flour to make a good thick roux. Season with salt and red pepper, and add some wine and lemon. Add this, with some button mushrooms that have been fried in butter, to the crab meat, and heat it. If you wish you can add some nice pieces of foie gras, a few spoonsful of petits pois, and some asparagus tips which have been previously boiled. Mix all these very carefully together, and sauté for a few minutes. Brown some breadcrumbs and sprinkle them on top, or grated Parmesan cheese can be used. Serve very hot with plain rice.

Scampi   *Scampi* have become increasingly popular in this country, and now that they can be bought in frozen form they are ideal for making something quick. You can use them either as a first course or for the main dish. In restaurants they often roll them in flour and egg and breadcrumbs and then fry in deep, very hot oil and serve with mustard sauce, which is nothing more than mayonnaise mixed with plenty of English mustard. I find the scampi too greasy fried, so I make them like this. Allow to de-freeze—this takes two or three hours—and then separate the scampi, looking out for any black spots and removing them. Add salt. Meanwhile cut up a small onion very finely, and fry it in butter in a saucepan until golden-brown. Add half a teaspoon of paprika, then put in the scampi and stir for five minutes, very carefully so as not to damage them. It may be better to shake the pan from time to time instead of using a spoon. Now pour in a good portion of thick cream. Do not let it boil, just simmer and serve immediately with boiled rice.

Scampi can be very good also if you just put them in hot butter, add salt, and cook for ten minutes. Sprinkle very finely chopped dill over them, and again serve with boiled rice.

The last time I was in Paris we went for lunch in a tiny restaurant in a small side-street, just because we happened to be there. The restaurant looked nothing from the outside, but we knew from experience that in France the most modest-looking establishment often has the best food. We were received by a charming woman—in England we would have called her pleasant and homely-looking and very friendly. We explained that we just wanted a bite, a little lunch and a glass of good wine, and we would like to leave it to her what to give us. This was not so hazardous as some of you may think. In my own business I never give more care and thought to an order, small or big, than when the customer tells me, "I leave it to you." The one who says that gets all that I have and my heart as well. So I said to this Frenchwoman, "We leave it to you." With a pleasant smile she disappeared.

About fifteen minutes later we each got a big plate of mussels, which she told me was called *Moules Gratinoc*. Each mussel was in a half-shell, and it was a wonderful dish. I have often made it since. Scrub a pint of mussels very thoroughly, then cook them in a cupful of white wine, with a few slices of onion, a carrot, celeriac, a leek, half a parsnip, and a little pepper. When the mussels open in the

Moules Gratinoc

steam, take them out of their shells and keep the liquid. Cream some butter with a lot of chopped parsley, a clove of garlic (which has to be pressed through a garlic presser), salt and pepper. Now place each mussel on a half-shell, sprinkle with the liquid in which the mussels were cooked, and cover with a layer of the savoury butter that you have just made. Sprinkle with grated cheese, and cook in a hot oven until brown. It is a really delicious first course.

If you want to know what to have after it—at this French restaurant the woman followed Moules Gratinoc with roast partridge with apple (see page 88). So we did not really have just the bite we asked for, but a marvellous feast.

Oysters   There is nothing much for me to say about *Oysters*, except that, to my regret, personally I cannot eat them raw. The last time I tried was when I was invited to dinner by a great gourmet, who ordered oysters for both of us as a matter of course. When I am a guest it is my strict rule to eat everything that is put before me—if I die afterwards, that is literally my funeral. So I struggled through those oysters, and it was the hardest work I have ever done in my life. My host said happily, "Isn't it wonderful to feel the whole sea in your mouth?" I thought it would be wonderful if I survived. I did not want to have the whole sea in my mouth, still less in my stomach. But, as you see, I lived to tell the tale.

I have already insulted the true gourmets with a recipe for oyster soup (see page 17), so I may as well be hung for a sheep as a lamb, as the English so picturesquely put it, and tell of one of the ways that I like oysters cooked.

Oysters à la   The dish is called *Oysters à la Favorite*. Immerse the oysters
Favorite   in boiling water for a short while, then mix with white cream sauce and put back in their empty shells. For the sauce make a simple Béchamel (see page 117) with the addition of a little fresh cream and a little of the water the oysters were boiled in. Cover with slices of truffle, sprinkle

with Parmesan cheese, and place in the oven to create a crust.

Now I think I have talked enough about fish, although I know I have only touched the fringe of the subject. Before I leave it I should like to tell one story that I heard when I stayed with some friends at Bognor Regis. They had lent their house to King George V after his illness—in fact I had the honour to sleep in a wonderful red Chinese bed where Queen Mary slept at that time. While Their Majesties were staying there the chef wanted some fish, and sent out for it to one of the local fishmongers. The fishmonger was very proud, and the next day he put out a poster which read, *"The King bought fish here"*. On the other side of the road another fishmonger, angry but quick, put out a poster reading, *"God Save the King!"*

CHAPTER FOUR

THE BEST MEAT IN THE WORLD

ONCE I read a book by a fashionable dietician who suggested that each bite should be chewed thirty-seven times. I cannot remember why he picked on this figure, but he said that if you ate in this way you would live for a very long time. I think you would have to, because you would need hours and hours for each meal if you really wanted to chew every bite thirty-seven times.

At the same time I am not in favour of swallowing food whole. I am sure you know already that it is important to eat in the right frame of mind—that if you eat in a good-humoured mood your digestive juices will work in the most effective way. But in my opinion the most important thing of all is to eat slowly and with your mind on what you are eating; and surely good food, well cooked, deserves this little compliment?

Women—as they will admit, if they are honest—cook mainly for men: for their husbands, their sons, and their male guests. The food men like best is meat—and the quality of meat in this country is the highest in the world. Every British housewife knows how to cook meat—to roast a joint of beef, or fry or grill a steak; but, once again, I think it is worth while to talk about other ways of cooking meat for a change.

Roast Beef (English) I myself roast beef in almost the traditional English way. I salt it very thoroughly; and before placing it in the roasting dish I put in a carrot, a piece of celeriac, half an onion, a clove of garlic, and two or three tomatoes, which

I fry together for two or three minutes; then I put in the meat. The only other thing I have to say about this justly famous dish is that I think it very important to have it on the table immediately it is ready. Beef is not good when it is kept, and should always be served very hot—rather let the guests wait for the roast beef than let the roast beef stand waiting for the guests.

For a change I sometimes roast beef in a way that was very popular in my parents' house. Take a piece of beef of about five or six pounds, and season with salt and paprika. Finely chop one large onion, and fry it; add two pounds of chopped mushrooms, season with salt and black pepper, and fry with the onion. Take two pounds of white bread dough (see standard household bread, page 150), or salty brioche (see page 156), and roll it out finger thick. Spread the mushroom and onion on it, then put on the meat. Cover the meat with the rolled-out dough, and put it in a roasting tin. Cover with some lard, and put in the oven. Baste frequently, and from time to time brush the dough with a piece of very cold butter. Cook for three and a half hours. If the dough becomes too brown, put a piece of greaseproof paper on it. With vegetables this is an excellent meal.

Roast Beef
(Hungarian)

I suppose that when we think of meat nearly all of us think first of beef, in a general way, and then of roast beef and beefsteak. When I think of *Steak* I think also of a friend who was one of the best doctors I have known. He was, indeed, a great doctor—and a great eater, too. He loved and understood food and wine.

Steak

Once he dined with us when there were about twelve persons at the table, and he entertained us all because, in addition to his other gifts, he was an excellent conversationalist. He told us that as a young doctor he was invited to a doctors' conference, and at their meeting they had a grand banquet. Several of the big shots made the usual after-dinner speeches. A very famous one was urged to make a speech as well. He got up and said, "I was told that an after-dinner speech should be short. I am afraid that I am going to have to disappoint you now. My speech will be very long, but it is not my fault." He took out a piece of paper and went on, "I shall read to you what Dr. Plesch"—that was the name of my friend—"has eaten at this excellent banquet"; and, as our friend admitted, the speech was very long indeed.

He came to visit me once during the last war, and I invited him to dinner because I had been lucky enough to obtain three lovely fillet steaks. When he arrived his first question was, "What will we have for dinner?" I told him that I had some very nice steaks. I said we would have foie gras with Melba toast first, and then the steaks. He asked whether I wouldn't mind if he cooked the steaks. I was delighted. He said, "Then let us first eat the goose liver, and then I will cook the steaks."

He ate very slowly, with great gusto, enjoying each mouthful and telling interesting stories all the time. He had been all over the world and had friends everywhere. One was the great Epstein, with whom he had a lively correspondence. His patients included kings and princes, and the poorest people, whom he treated free of charge. We were so busy listening to him that when he had finished the foie gras the whole thing had disappeared and we hadn't touched it. I didn't mind, although I had an idea my husband was a little bit sore about it because he loves foie gras. Anyway, we then all went in the kitchen. The vegetables and everything had been prepared. Our guest took a very thick frying pan, put on the highest gas flame, and put a good amount of rough salt and roughly ground black pepper on both sides of the steak. He then put the steaks in with no fat whatsoever, and cooked each side for five minutes. The steaks were about one inch thick. I never ate better.

Porterhouse   I think *Porterhouse* is an excellent steak. I cook it in very little fat for five minutes each side. But first I salt and black pepper it—in spite of the belief that salt stiffens the steak. If I find the steak does not look as I like it, I first rub in French mustard and then cover with olive oil, and let it stand for one or two hours; after that I just fry it.

To prepare *Mignon Steaks*—a great delicacy—soak the individual portions in red wine for twenty-four hours, and drain; sauté onions and carrots in butter; gently grill the steaks, and add grilled mushrooms. Serve with the vegetables, straw potatoes, and haricots verts, and a sauce piquante (see page 119).

Mignon Steak

My younger son and his wife often come to stay with me for week-ends, and I use them as guinea-pigs to try out new dishes that I have thought up during sleepless nights.

Recently I gave them something new with beef, which they both like. First I bought some porterhouse steak— and I asked one of the assistants, who is a great friend, to give me very thin slices indeed. He did a very good job, and from one thin porterhouse steak I got two very large but thin slices. At the same time I bought some nice calf's brains and half a pound of calf's liver.

How Green Steak

When I got home I salted and black-peppered both sides of the meat. Then I boiled the brains in salt water and took off the skin. Next I washed a little rice very thoroughly and put it in salted water to boil for five minutes. Meanwhile I sautéd a small chopped onion in a little lard, put in the brains, and added three whole eggs. While this was cooking—it only takes a few minutes—I put into the oven a baking tin containing some lard, a carrot, a parsnip, a shallot, a clove of garlic, some celery, and three or four tomatoes, and let them brown.

Now I spread the brains and egg on the meat, and then put on this a very thin slice of the liver, and finally added the cooked rice. I rolled it together and secured it with cocktail-sticks, and then put it in the baking tin with the vegetables, which were now nice and brown. There I browned the rolled meat on both sides, and then poured some beef stock on it and let it simmer until tender.

The last stage was to take out the rolled meat and put it

in a serving dish, where it was kept warm while the vegetables were passed through a sieve. I mixed a little cream with the resulting purée, which I poured on the meat roll and served very hot. It was quite a success. Everybody liked it, and called it *How Green Steak* after the name of my house.

Boeuf à la Mode (Two Recipes)

Another of my favourite beef dishes is filet de *Boeuf à la Mode*. Put a piece of fillet of beef, well larded, in a casserole, pour a small glass of brandy over it, and leave for three hours. Then add some red wine and one diced carrot, a chopped onion, some peppercorns, and a bay leaf, and leave for a further three hours, turning the meat over twice to be sure the flavour penetrates. Next take the beef out, season with salt and pepper, and put in a very hot oven, adding the diced vegetables. Roast till it is well coloured on both sides, then add the wine and brandy and a little stock and finish off with the lid on. Strain off the gravy. Garnish the dish with braised button onions, mushrooms, carrots, etc.

II

I have also had *Boeuf à la Mode* consisting of fillet of beef with strips of smoked bacon. Roasted in butter add white wine and slices of bacon, ham, and veal, all served in a large dish with brandy poured into the sauce. This was excellent with young pear-shaped carrots and very fine petits pois, tiny onions, and button mushrooms.

Boiled Beef

Boiled Beef is what I would call a manly dish. It is especially popular among very masculine men. But it is not exclusive to them—indeed, even I, who am supposed to be a very feminine type of woman, enjoy boiled beef and regard it as difficult to beat.

As always, the dish depends absolutely on the kind of meat you have to boil. It has to be first-class beef, I should say from a fattened ox. Which part of the ox you select is a matter of taste. Some say the shin is the best, others say the breast; I have been told the juicy neck part is the right one, but from my experience it can also be part of the leg. The main thing is that it should be a good large

piece. You cannot make good boiled beef from little bits—
you must have a large joint.

My father's favourite lunch was boiled beef, preceded
by the soup in which the meat was cooked. Usually he
praised my mother's cooking—often he used to tell her
that she should open a sanatorium for people with stomach
troubles, because she would cure everyone with her cooking—but in his opinion her boiled beef was never very
satisfactory. He did not blame her for this, nor did he think
there was anything she could do about it. He said it was
only possible to make good boiled beef if a huge piece was
cooked, otherwise the meat became too dry. If we were
going to have boiled beef my mother would order six or
seven pounds of beef, five or six pounds of bones, and one
huge marrow bone. A restaurant would order forty or
fifty pounds. The best ox-meat was always sent from
Budapest to Vienna, and my father often took the trouble
to travel to Vienna to go to Maisel and Shaden's restaurant
to eat really good boiled beef. Personally, I thought our
own boiled beef was good. The marrow bone was a great
source of joy if at the last moment it was placed on the
table by someone who knew how to handle it correctly so
that the marrow came out in one big lump. This was put
on hot toast with a little salt and paprika, and was regarded as a great delicacy.

I boil beef by putting the meat in salted hot water,
boiling till nearly tender, and then putting into the liquid
all the vegetables I can lay my hands on—carrots, parsnips, celery, celeriac, a very small piece of turnip (it has
such an overwhelming flavour), a small piece of pimento,
two or three tomatoes, one clove of garlic, an onion, a
leek, a small piece of cabbage, one or two Brussels sprouts,
a small piece of Savoy cabbage, kohl-rabi, a piece of lettuce,
four or five black peppercorns, and a very little saffron.
You must be careful with saffron: a little gives a very
pleasant additional flavour, but if it is overdone it spoils
the whole soup and meat.

I generally serve the soup with some kind of garnish and with the cooked vegetables in it, and then serve the boiled meat with a good hot sauce.

The cheaper parts of the ox are, of course, suitable for making stews. If Hungary is known for any dish it is the *Goulash* world-famous *Goulash*, which is just like your stew except that we first fry onions with paprika, and sometimes add cream when the stew is ready. We make goulash with beef, veal, chicken, or lamb. One of my favourite goulashes is made with lamb, and I will give the recipe when I have finished with the ox and the calf.

Swedish Stew Goulash is by no means the only kind of stew I make. I ate a very good stew in Sweden, which I sometimes cook myself at home. For this you need about three or four pounds of meat, preferably beef, which you should rub well with pepper and salt and hard frozen lard. Put in a casserole, cook in the oven, turning it, and then pour on it a cup of good stock. Add some pieces of fat pork, two onions, four anchovies, one bay leaf, two tablespoons of vinegar or red wine, and a small glass of brandy. Cook until the meat is tender. Mix three to four tablespoons of flour with a quarter of a pint of cream, add this to the gravy, and serve.

Veal In Hungary we used to eat a lot of *Veal*. It was just as good there as it is in France and Italy today—they do not kill the calves very young, but young enough. Personally, I think veal has a very pleasant flavour and is mostly tender, and it can be cooked in so many ways. The most famous is probably the Wiener Schnitzel, which I do in exactly the same way as fried chicken (see page 70).

Another good way is to take a thin slice of veal, salt it well, rub in a little black pepper, put a piece of butter on it, and grill on each side for five or six minutes. Then place a slice of ham on the veal, and a thin slice of Gruyère cheese on the ham, and grill until the cheese melts. Serve immediately.

Veal Carmen In Italy once, in a charming and elegant restaurant, I ate a dish that was named on the very artistic menu as

Veal Carmen. I cannot imagine why. But it was excellent. The veal looked like Wiener Schnitzel, but tasted better, and it was served in a dish of spaghetti garnished with tomato sauce and Parmesan cheese. You can make it yourself.

Salt and black-pepper both sides of the veal, and fry it on both sides for four to five minutes. Let it cool, and cover on both sides with a very well-cooked Béchamel sauce (see page 117). This sauce must be thick enough to cover the veal slices all over. Now dip the veal in egg-yolk and breadcrumbs, and fry. Meanwhile cook the spaghetti, and then pile it up in a dish. Place the veal slices round it, and serve with tomato sauce and Parmesan cheese.

For *Roast Leg of Veal* in Hungary we used a small but very tasty and aromatic yellow mushroom that unfortunately I have never seen here; but you can replace it with an ordinary mushroom. First chop an onion very finely, and put it in a frying pan, then add one pound of chopped mushrooms, salt and pepper. When the onions are golden-brown take the pan off the heat. Mix three eggs with a quarter of a pint of cream, and add to the mushrooms and onions. Now take a small leg of veal—if it is too big take out the middle part, called the nut. Bone the veal, lay it out flat and spread it with the mushroom mixture. Then roll up the veal and tie it firmly with string. Into a large baking tin put a good tablespoon of lard, one carrot cut in four pieces, one parsnip cut in pieces, a piece of celery, a piece of celeriac, two or three tomatoes, and one onion or leek. Roast for a few minutes in the oven, and then put in the rolled veal. Brown on both sides. Baste with white wine. Cook under a cover for two and a half to three hours—until the veal is tender; I cannot give the exact time because it always depends on the age of the calf.

Roast Leg of Veal

A good roast can be made with *Breast of Veal*, which is very cheap. Buy a half of a veal breast. It you don't

Roast Breast of Veal

know how to make a pocket in the meat, ask the butcher to do it for you—I find that a nice smile goes a long way with the butcher. Wash two pounds of spinach, salt it and cook in very little water for ten minutes. Meanwhile take three egg-yolks, mix in a piece of butter, half a pound of breadcrumbs, black pepper, salt and one or two tablespoons of cream. Beat the whites of the eggs until stiff. Chop quite a lot of parsley. Drain the spinach very well—it should not be watery—and mix with the egg-whites and chopped parsley, then put this on the bottom of the pocket in the breast of veal. With a spoon put the egg-and-breadcrumbs mixture in on top of the spinach. Sew up the pocket, and put the stuffed veal in a baking tin with a piece of lard. Baste it with stock of white wine, and roast until tender.

Veal with White Sauce   Nothing can be much better than *Veal Cooked in White Sauce*. First make a good stock from all the available veal bones, then cut the meat into small pieces. Take a heavy pan, and put in it six ounces of butter for two pounds of veal. Salt the meat and put it in the hot butter. Roast until golden-yellow, then sprinkle on it two tablespoons of rice or potato flour. Add a little stock from time to time, and let it simmer slowly. Put in a clove of garlic when it starts to simmer if you like, but be careful to take it out carefully after half an hour as the garlic should not break. You can add white wine or lemon juice, or both, before serving, and put in chopped parsley generously. Serve with boiled rice or noodles or spaghetti.

Veal Goulash   The bony part of veal, or the lower part of the leg or breast, is good for making *Veal Goulash*. There is no need for me to describe how this is made, as it is exactly the same as chicken goulash (see page 72).

Meat Balls   For making *Meat Balls* I think veal is best—unless, of course, you use breast of turkey; but who will sacrifice that for minced meat? So take a pound of minced veal—if you like you can add half a pound of minced pork—and mix it with two whole eggs, one ounce of butter, very little cream, salt and black pepper, plenty of chopped fresh parsley, and enough breadcrumbs to bind the mixture without making it too stiff. Wet your hand, and then mould the mixture into nice small round balls. Put them in breadcrumbs in a wooden bowl. Heat quite a bit of lard in a frying-pan, and when it is very hot put in the meat balls. They should swim in the fat and fry until a golden colour.

If you like you can make a small loaf of the same *Veal Loaf* mixture, and roast it in the oven until nice and brown, basting from time to time. You can make a lot of combinations for minced meat loaf. Before cooking you can put in the middle a hard-boiled egg, or pistachio nuts or any kind of sausage. Minced meat loaf looks very nice when you cut it in slices.

In Bavaria—where I go often to Munich—the beer cellars *Calves'* and beer houses serve thousands of *Calves' Knuckles*—so *Knuckles* many, indeed, that you would think Bavarian calves have more than four legs. The Germans just love this good and large portion of meat that is comparatively cheap. Calves' knuckles are very easy to cook. You just wash the knuckle and salt it well, rub in a little paprika, and put in a roasting tin with lard. Roast until brown, crisp, and tender.

And now lamb . . . *Roast Lamb*, which, I am sure, *Roast Lamb* everyone in this country can cook better than I do. You can get a good roast lamb or chops in almost any restaurant. I would only like to suggest, if I may, that you use a little seasoning on your meat before cooking—salt, paprika, and pepper. Also if you roast your lamb with some carrots, onions, a whole clove of garlic, one tomato, parsnips, and celery, you will find it most tasty. When I cook a leg of lamb I do this—and on the last lap of the roasting I pour red wine or port on it, and find that I have a better joint and a better gravy.

In England the lamb is always very good—especially if it is a good English lamb—and all parts of it are excellent. In Hungary we could enjoy only the very young baby lamb, for when it was a little older—four to six months old—it had a very strong mutton smell which few people liked. But the baby lamb was wonderful, and I still like it best of all. It is most delicious when just plain roasted, and that was how we had our first baby lamb of the year on 2nd March last—a very early day for this delicacy.

I salted and rubbed some paprika in the lamb's ribs, and then put into the roasting dish one carrot cut into four pieces, half a parsnip, half a piece of celery, and half a celeriac, all cut in pieces, a leek, and half an onion. Adding some lard, I put this in the oven. I prepared the vegetables first because the baby lamb does not need more than an hour. When this was ready I put in the lamb, with a few dots of lard on it, and let it roast on both sides for a few minutes, then added a little hot water—about two or three tablespoons—and roasted the lamb for fifty to sixty minutes. I basted it often, to make it brown and crisp. I think it is a wonderful roast with new potatoes and green vegetables, the best being a creamy spinach.

Lamb Stew From the bony part of the baby lamb I make a stew, and this is my husband's favourite dish. He thinks it the king of all the meat dishes. You can make it with lamb cutlets or, even better, breast of lamb—but the lamb must be really young. That is why Easter is the best time for this lamb stew, which is one form of the world-famous Hungarian goulash.

Take four or five onions, chop them up well, and put them in a large stew-pan or saucepan with lard. Cook until they are golden-brown. Press in two or three cloves of garlic. Do this with a "garlic press", an American gadget which I think is a great invention—I bought mine in the United States years ago, but you can get it in this country now. You have to be very careful with garlic: it should never burn, because if it does it has a very bad flavour. After pressing in the garlic, add two tablespoons of Hungarian paprika, stir, and immediately put in the meat, which should have been cut into three-inch pieces. Stir for a few minutes, salt well, and add two or three whole tomatoes and a teaspoon of carraway seed. Stir again, and pour some water on it—about two pints, but it depends how much meat you have. Let it cook for about fifteen or twenty minutes, then add quite a lot of peeled potatoes cut lengthwise. Stir in, and when the potatoes are ready the dish is ready. The whole process should take at least an hour, depending on the age of the animal, and it is really the best stew you can have. Try it: it is worth while.

There was one way—and only one—that my father liked mutton, and in Hungary it was really mutton and not lamb. It was stewed with millet. *Mutton Stew*

Again fry four or five large onions in lard until golden-yellow. Press through two to four cloves of garlic, add two or three tablespoons of paprika, then put in small mutton pieces. Salt well, and stir for two to four minutes; then add enough water to cover. Put on the lid, and let the meat boil for one or two hours, until it is tender but not quite ready. If the water evaporates add some more hot water. Then wash one pound of yellow millet, add to the stew, and let it boil for another twenty minutes. It is a good dish.

Pork is a delicious meat, and a pig is an exciting, intelligent animal, very much misunderstood and wrongly judged. It is fussy what it eats and especially what it drinks, but most of all it keeps its bedroom clean. The pig is not a dirty animal but a very wise animal. You see it sometimes giving itself a bad name by rolling in the mud, but that is something we do too; except that mostly we travel a long way and spend a small fortune in trying to cure our rheumatism with a mud bath. The pig knows that Mother Earth is good for everything, so it takes a mud bath to prevent or cure its rheumatism without making any expensive journeys at all. *Pork*

Pig meat is unequalled by any other meat—for what other animal gives you such a variety of good food? First there is the ham, which you enjoy when you are well and which you can eat if you are ill. Then there is your daily delight for breakfast with your eggs—bacon. There is the great variety of fresh and smoked meat called pork—and, finally, the many different kinds of pork sausages that can be eaten any time of the day, from breakfast till supper at midnight.

The quality of pork and bacon depends on how the pig is fed, starting when it is a little suckling or even before. In Hungary the pigs were fed first with maize and bran. Now, of course, the feeding of pigs is perfectly scientific. The animal is fed for the purpose for which it is wanted—for meat, bacon, fat, or lard.

To kill a pig in a house is a most exciting occasion. There is a Chinese proverb that says, "If you want to be happy for one day, marry. If you want to be happy for two days, kill a pig. If you want to be happy for a lifetime, be a gardener." I would not like to swear that this quotation is exact, but I promise that you will be happy for two or three days when you kill a pig.

The actual killing, of course, is done by an expert, and no one else takes part. In our house this was done off-stage, and the first we knew about it was when they brought in the blood, which was very much needed for one kind of sausage. Killing a pig is a very economical matter, for you can eat everything except the hair—I think it is called bristle in the pig world. You could use this too, but for the best of the bacon it is burnt off the pig. I remember watching the big straw fire they used to take off the bristle. Then they started to scrape and clean the pig, and when it was beautifully clean they brought it into the kitchen. That was when the fun really started.

First we opened the pig, and took out the intestines, which went immediately into salted water and were washed and cleaned very efficiently until they had a nice clean smell and appearance. Then the pig was cut in pieces, and that was really very expert work. The two back legs were put aside for the ham, and the rest for whatever purpose it was required.

A big part of the meat was used for sausage-making. *Sausages* We made four kinds of sausages. First there was pork-meat sausage, for which no ingredients were used other than the pork, water, and seasoning. Next came the black sausage, which you very wrongly call black pudding. It is not a pudding at all, it is a sausage made with blood, and it should not be insulted with the name of pudding. Thirdly there was the liver sausage, and lastly the sausage made of the lights. Sometimes for fun I make three of these kinds of sausage in my kitchen. I cannot get the blood to make the black sausage, but I do the others with artificial skin.

For the *Meat Sausage* I buy seven pounds of pork, half *Meat Sausage* lean and the other half fatty, and mince it, but not very fine. Then I add salt, red pepper, black pepper, and some garlic. I don't like garlic pieces in a sausage, therefore I take two or three cloves of garlic and put them in one pint of water for half an hour, and use only the water and leave the garlic. If you don't want garlic at all you can use lemon-peel, which is very good and has an interesting flavour. This sausage is good when freshly roasted in the oven; or you can send it to be smoked, and after it has been in smoke for three or four days you can hang it up and keep it for quite a while. Then you don't roast it but just boil it in water.

For the *Liver Sausage*, boil the pig's liver in salted *Liver Sausage* water, then pass it through a fine mincing machine. Boil part of the neck of the pig—the fatty part—and cut it in very small cubes. For two pounds of liver use ten ounces of this fat. Add salt and black pepper. Put the skin on the mincing machine, adjust it, and make the sausage by pressing the meat through the machine into the skin. When it is ready, boil it for a few minutes in the same water in which the liver was boiled, then roast it in the oven.

Light
Sausage

The lights make an excellent sausage. One pig's lights are boiled in the same way as the liver and minced. Use two pounds of lights to one pound of bacon cut in small pieces. Then take one onion, cut it very small, and fry it in lard until golden-brown. Boil some rice—half a pound for two pounds of lights—for five or six minutes, and then mix this with the lights and onions. Add salt and black pepper. Push the mixture into the sausage skin, and boil it for a few minutes in the same water as before. Roast in the oven.

You can keep the liver sausages and light sausages for only a few days in the refrigerator. They cannot be kept long because they are not smoked. It is a little trouble to make these sausages, but it is worth it, and if you like to have a barbecue party they will be an enormous success.

Brawn

From the pig's head we used to make what we called pork cheese. Here it is called *Brawn*. I make it sometimes, when I can get a pig's head. Clean this, taking care to remove all the bristle, and remove all the teeth. Cut the head into two or three pieces, and boil until tender in salted water with one bay leaf, a few black peppercorns, a carrot, a piece of celery, an onion, and a clove of garlic. It is a good idea to boil the pig's legs or trotters with the head, as these have a very good jellifying effect. Take out all the meat and remove all the bones. Reduce the liquid. Cut the meat in one-inch pieces, and put in a china mould or a large pudding basin. Season with salt and red and black pepper, and add more garlic if you like it. Skim all the fat from the reduced liquid, and pour in the dish. It will be jellified in a few hours, and you can keep it for days. It can be served in slices with some nice salad.

From some parts of the pig we made roast pork. From the bony part we made boiled pork or soup. Usually we took part of the meat off the bony pieces for making sausages, and boiled the rest in exactly the same way as we boiled beef (see page 54). Boiled pork with apple purée and horse-radish mixed is one of the most delightful dishes which men especially love.

The loin of pork can be used in many ways. When we killed more than one pig we put the loins in pickle sometimes, just like the ham but for a shorter time—about eight to ten days. Then we smoked it, and when cooked it was better than any ham.

Here is an interesting recipe for a roll of fresh *Loin of Pork*. First, one day before, put half a pound of Californian prunes in warm water and let them swell. Now take three or four pounds of pork loin, and rub in salt and paprika. With a sharp-pointed knife make a hole in the loin, and insert the stoned prunes. Tie with a piece of string. Brown on all sides in the oven, and pour over some hot stock. Cover with a lid, and simmer in a low heat for about an hour and a half or until tender. When ready, put on a hot dish and remove the string. Cut the meat loose from the backbone, and slice. It is a very decorative and tasty dish.

Loin of Pork

An excellent mousse can be made with smoked ham. Boil the ham, and make the mousse from the stock by adding cream, gelatine (see page 26), and minced ham. Line a mould with liquid aspic jelly and lay a few slices of tomatoes and gherkins on the bottom. Pour the mixture into the mould, and place in the refrigerator to set. When firm, turn out on to a dish that has been covered with lettuce leaves. Decorate with slices of rolled ham. Serve with Cumberland or redcurrant sauce (see page 122). Remember to let the aspic set before adding the mousse.

Ham Mousse

The pig-killing season in Hungary began before Christmas and went on until February, and some houses with big families killed as many as four pigs during this time. We had no refrigerators then, so we had to depend on the cold weather to preserve the meat. That is why February was the latest month for killing pigs.

At the end of the season every family invited their friends for the so-called *Disznotor*, or Pig Festival Dinner. The meal was composed of dishes made from the delicacies of the pig—fresh sausages, fresh pork cutlets, sauerkraut stuffed with a lot of pork, and, as a special delicacy, the pig's head. Fashions changed, and clever and imaginative hostesses combined all kinds of things with the products of the pig, and it became a competition between the hostesses for the distinction of giving the most original dinner.

We made many more interesting dishes with pork, but I shall describe only one more, and that is the stuffed suckling pig.

The *Suckling Pig* was the festival food on New Year's Eve in Hungary. I could never find out whence or why, but New Year's Eve would not have been complete without it. The little pig needs to be very young—not more than six weeks at the most; over two months it loses its distinctive flavour and becomes a simple pig. Of course there is not a lot of meat on one suckling pig, but its flesh is delicious and tender, the skin is brittle and crisp, and makes a perfect and lovely-looking dish.

Open and clean the suckling pig very thoroughly, and take out all the bones except from the feet and head. Salt and pepper very well, and pour brandy over it. Let it stand for one hour. Fry one finely chopped onion, and add to it the pig's liver, half a pound of calf's liver, the pig's heart, two hard-boiled eggs—all finely chopped—and some chopped parsley. Mix all together with two raw eggs. Moisten with a little white wine. Put all this in the suckling pig, and then sew it up. Place the stuffed suckling pig in a large roasting pan. Put lard on it and baste from time to time as it roasts. It needs about three hours, and must be brown and very crisp. Serve with a lemon in its mouth.

When the clock struck twelve on Sylvester, as we called New Year's Eve, a man brought in a beautiful live little pig with a big bow round its neck, and everybody touched it. It meant good luck for the New Year. Then a black-faced handsome chimney sweep with a black moustache came our way the same evening—it was usually arranged so, and then our hopes rose and we were assured that our dreams would come true in the New Year. It was so good to believe. I still love to go to a fortune-teller, and I always pay a visit if I hear of one, however far away. I like it even better if it is far away—I take the trouble to go, and I always believe what the fortune-teller says; for fortune-tellers wisely never say anything but what you want to hear.

CHAPTER FIVE

THE POULTRY YARD

CHICKEN is the best invalid food, and to stimulate a feeble appetite there is nothing like the white meat of a young chicken. It is one of the lightest meats, one of the most nutritious, and surely one of the tastiest. It saddens me to hear people saying, as I often do hear them, "Oh, I am fed up with chicken—we get it always and everywhere." Because for me chicken is a festive dish. In my childhood on every important occasion chicken was one of the main dishes in the very best chosen menus; and in my mother's house chicken was always a wonderful dish. It looked like a still-life picture, and tasted even better than it looked. The variety of ways in which it was prepared and cooked was really unbelievable. If we had been lucky enough to have chicken every day I am sure we would never have been "fed up".

That reminds me of a story I read somewhere about Napoleon, who also got tired of chicken. He complained about it to one of his courtiers, a famous gourmet and noble aristocrat. He was fed up with it, Napoleon said, because it always had the same taste. The noble gourmet answered that he was willing to wager his title that he could serve the Emperor with chickens twice a day for a whole year and that the taste would always be quite different and new. According to the story the noble gourmet kept his rank.

Chicken Suprême

For *Chicken Suprême* you should use a very young spring chicken, weighing two or two and a half pounds. Salt it well, and rub in a little paprika. Roast in a good warm oven in butter—about half or three-quarters of an ounce—

68

with a little stock or, failing that, water, and baste from time to time. As an extra, toast some thin slices of white bread, and put on each one a slice of foie gras with a truffle in the middle. Make a sauce from two ounces of butter and a tablespoon of flour, stir it for a minute, season with salt and a little white pepper, add a glass of white wine, and cook for three to five minutes. Lastly add a tablespoon of brandy. Before serving, stir in it a quarter of a pint of cream worked together with one egg-yolk. Taste and adjust the seasoning accordingly. Put the foie gras on toast on to a large dish, and place a piece of chicken on each piece of toast. Pour the sauce on it, but it should not cover all the chicken, only the side.

Here is another recipe for *Spring Chicken*, again with foie gras. First cook together vegetables—spring onions, spring carrots, peas, and two peeled tomatoes—very slowly, with sufficient chicken stock to cover. Add salt, a teaspoon of sugar, and an ounce of butter. Cook uncovered until the liquid is reduced to a coating glaze. Sauté the chicken in butter until tender—about twenty minutes. Garnish with the glazed spring vegetables and some foie gras. *(margin: Spring Chicken Sauté)*

My own most recent chicken dish is *Spring Chicken* stuffed with veal and foie gras. The chicken should be small but plump. Clean it thoroughly—there is nothing so unpleasant as that feather flavour in birds—and then cut down the back and take out all the inside. With a very sharp-pointed knife remove all the bones except the lower part of the leg-bone, which must be left. Then mince some veal, and mix with it salt, pepper, egg, and a very little cream. Work it together well, then roll out into the shape of a pancake and pack a piece of foie gras in it. Put it in the chicken, salt and pepper it inside and outside, and roll the bird so that it looks like a whole chicken. You have to shape it cleverly. Brush it with chicken fat if you have any, if not a good pork lard will do. Put it in a baking tin and place in a very hot oven for fifty-five to sixty minutes. *(margin: Stuffed Spring Chicken)*

It has to look cheerful and rosy. Serve with new potatoes and cucumber salad.

Poulet à la Clare

For *Poulet à la Clare*, cut two spring chickens—about two and a half pounds each—into four pieces, and season with salt and black pepper. Then put them in a pan with a little fresh pork fat, and brown on both sides. Let them cook about a quarter of an hour, turning the pieces from time to time; then add four or five tablespoons of brandy, light it, and shake the pan until the flame dies. Add four nice-sized chopped shallots and plenty of chopped parsley, a little chopped thyme and one wineglass of white wine. Cover the saucepan, and cook until the chicken is tender. When cooked, take out the chicken pieces and arrange in a warm dish. Add a small cup of thick cream to the sauce, but don't let it boil. Pour the sauce over the chicken, and serve with spaghetti.

Fried Chicken

Fried Chicken is a dish that appears on the menu at any festival all over the world. When I was in America I was introduced to chicken Maryland—as a surprise it was a failure, but I did not complain when it turned out to be nothing else but our old friend fried chicken. Usually it is served with fried banana, but I prefer it with a ring of pineapple and a slice of peach.

In many cookery books you will find the statement that the chicken ought to be bought a day before and kept in the refrigerator overnight. Our cook in Hungary had quite different ideas. When a coach rolled into our yard with unexpected guests she just looked to see how many there were and then ordered the kitchen maid: "Run and bring four"—or however many were needed, according to the number of guests—"young spring chickens". Off ran the kitchen-maid, a little girl of about fourteen who was terrified of Cook, and in a few minutes the chickens had been killed, plucked, washed and salted and cut into about eight pieces, according to their size. A chicken should be not more than two or two and a half pounds.

Our cook sprinkled the pieces of chicken with a very

little flour, dipped them in lightly beaten egg, and then rolled them in very fine white breadcrumbs. In a very large pot she heated enough fresh lard for the chicken pieces to swim in the deep, very hot fat. She put the pieces in the fat one by one, then put the pot on a lower heat, covered it with a lid, and let the chicken fry for ten or fifteen minutes. Then she turned the pieces over and let them fry slowly until they were a lovely golden brown colour.

We children, when we smelt the wonderful aroma of the fried chicken, ran to the kitchen. Our cook—one of the most interesting characters of my childhood—was tall, big, and firm, and all the other servants trembled at her harsh ways and words; but she was a sweet, kind person to us children, and she would do everything to please us. So when we ran into the kitchen, each of us got a large leg of fried chicken—in Hungary the leg was considered the best part, not the breast as here.

When my mother came out to see whether everything was well on the way for the meal, and found us each having a large piece of a chicken, she asked the cook, "What will you serve to the guests?" The cook answered, "What do I care about any guests? First come the children, and what is left the guests can have." In her heart my mother agreed. Anyway, she knew that our cook had seen to it that not only the guests but she herself would have enough of this delicious fresh fried chicken—or, if you like the name better, chicken Maryland. Our cook served it with new potatoes, and cucumber salad made with wine vinegar, a pinch of sugar, salt of course, and sour cream. It was a heavenly meal.

My father had a friend who was a great gourmet and a big eater—two things that do not always go together. My father asked him once how many pieces of fried chicken he could eat. He looked at the smoke of his after-dinner cigar and said, "You don't eat fried chicken by the piece. You eat it for half an hour, one hour, two hours—it depends."

I learnt a very good way of cooking chicken at the
Palace Hotel at St. Moritz. If I remember rightly the chef
Poulet au Vin   called it *Poulet au Vin*. Here is the recipe.

Bone the chicken, then cut it into pieces; if you have
about five and half pounds, make six or eight pieces. Take
a stewpan large enough for the amount of chicken, and
melt in it a quarter of a pound of chicken fat or butter. Salt
the pieces of chicken, and put them in the pan one by one
when the fat is very hot. Cook over a hot flame. When
the chicken pieces are golden brown, add a small chopped
onion and six or eight mushrooms. Cook for another five
to eight minutes, then sprinkle on the chicken a teaspoon
of potato flour and a good glass of white wine. Cook until
tender. If the sauce is too thick, add some chicken stock,
which you should always have ready. Take another pan,
and put into it long thin slices of bacon and one slice of
cooked tongue cut in very long thin strips. Sauté this, but
do not make it too crisp. Finally put the bacon and tongue
on the chicken and serve with roast potatoes and creamed
spinach.

Of all the different ways of cooking chicken—
and there really must be hundreds—none can compare,
Chicken   for me, with our *Chicken Paprika or Gaulash*, a traditional
Goulash   Hungarian dish. It should be young and well fed, with
a nice white breast; as, indeed, should all fowl, very
young chickens, including boiling fowl for making chicken
soup.

For a six-pound chicken take five very large onions,
chop them finely, and fry them in chicken fat or lard until
they are a golden colour. Add two tablespoons of paprika,
and stir it with the onions; then put in the chicken, cut in
eight or ten pieces, and one clove of finely crushed garlic.
Brown the chicken on both sides. Put in two or three
tomatoes or a spoonful of tomato purée, and half a green
chopped pimento, if it is in season. Cover the pan, and
cook for fifteen minutes. Add a quarter of a pint of chicken
stock and cook until tender, then add a quarter of a pint

of very thick cream. It should not be allowed to boil after adding the cream. Serve with dumplings (see page 144), noodles, or boiled potatoes.

When I first went to America, an American friend told me I would have to try the very famous *Chicken à la King*. This, like Maryland chicken, is claimed as an American national dish. Again like Maryland chicken, I had had it before, almost the same, but under a different name. We used to have it—and still do—when someone in the house is not very well.

Chicken à la King

To make our chicken dish for the invalid, first make a roux with a quarter of a pound of butter and an ounce of flour. Stir for a few minutes. Do not brown—it must stay white. Pour half a pint of chicken stock in to it, stirring all the time. It should not get lumpy. Then add the breast and wing of a young chicken cut in pieces, with salt and, if liked, a little white pepper. Cook for fifteen minutes, then add half a pint of white wine. Let it boil covered for another fifteen minutes, and then cook until tender. Sprinkle plenty of chopped parsley on the top, and serve with boiled rice.

When I make Chicken à la King I start in the same way as above, and add very white champignon mushrooms— about half a pound—cut in slices, together with fresh pimentos, red, yellow, and green, very finely sliced, and a little mace. Before serving, mix two egg-yolks with three tablespoons of cream and some chopped parsley, and pour over the chicken. Again serve with rice.

Chicken à la King can also be made with a good boiling fowl. Cook it in a little water with salt, peppercorns, a carrot, an onion, half a clove of garlic, a tomato, a sprig of parsley, and a sprig of celery. When cooked, pull the meat off the bones and cut up small and put into a casserole. Now make a sauce by melting a little butter and adding flour and finally the strained liquor from the chicken. Let it boil for a minute, then add one gill of cream, a few cooked sliced mushrooms, a few green peas (cooked first, unless tinned), and a red pimento cooked and cut up small, and pour over the chicken.

I have eaten many good chicken dishes in France, and one of the best of them was at the Carlton Hotel in Cannes. Here is the recipe.

Stuffed Chicken　　Take a chicken of five to six pounds, and stuff it with chopped and sautéd onions, some white breadcrumbs soaked in milk, the liver of the bird fried with chopped ham and chopped parsley and chopped tarragon, half a clove of garlic pressed through the garlic presser, and salt and black pepper, all mixed with one or two whole eggs. Put into a large soup saucepan, and add about three quarts of water, a piece of beef, all the giblets, some smoked ham, about half a pound of carrots, parsnips, celeriac, celery, leeks, onions, one bay leaf, and chopped parsley. If these vegetables are not available you can replace them with any other vegetables. Bring to the boil, and cook for twenty minutes. Skim a few times, then add the stuffed chicken and let it simmer very slowly for two and a half to three and a half hours or until it is tender. Mix a sauce of one ounce of butter and a little rice flour, let it brown for only a few minutes, then add some of the soup in which the stuffed chicken has boiled. Thicken this sauce with an egg-yolk and fresh thick cream and a little lemon juice according to your taste. Season, and add a little sugar if you like it.

This one dish makes the soup, meat, and sauce. Serve the chicken with the sauce and the other meat. The best is to cover the whole chicken with the sauce. Strain the soup, and serve with the boiled vegetables, which should be served cut very fine.

Chicken Curry　　To make a *Chicken Curry*, boil one or two medium-sized chickens until tender. To make the sauce, if you use two chickens you want two or three medium-sized onions, which you chop finely and put in a large saucepan with six or seven ounces of lard, some chopped celery, a bay leaf, two tablespoons of finely chopped chutney, two diced apples, half a pound of bacon, quite a lot of chopped parsley, and four tablespoons of flour. Mix these well together, and cook on a high flame for ten minutes. Add two cloves of garlic which have been pressed through a garlic press, a little powdered maize, and two teaspoons of curry powder. Mix well, and cook again for a few minutes. Then add one quart of the broth in which the chickens were boiled, season again if necessary, and cook slowly for an hour. Take the meat off the boiled chickens, mince it, and place it in another saucepan. Strain the sauce over this. Let it boil for about eight or ten minutes, and then add one pint of thick cream. After the cream has been added it must not boil any more—just heat it. Serve very hot with plain boiled rice.

One of the most interesting chicken dishes I have had was the famous *Pastilla* (or bistaela), which I ate with my son in a restaurant in Marrakesh. We had to sit on very low divans at very low tables, and before the meal was served two Arab girls in lovely dresses brought hand-bowls with warm water, soap, and clean towels, so that we could wash our hands before starting to eat. We had no spoons or forks, but had to eat with our fingers from the same dish.

Pastilla

To a certain extent it was like an English pie. The Arabs fill it with either chicken or pigeon—for me it must be chicken, because pigeon is one thing I simply cannot eat: I do not know why, but perhaps it is because as a child I used to keep pigeons as pets. Anyway, if you use chicken you simply make it like a stew. Start with fried onions, a little carrot and celery, some sliced pimento, and slices of ham and bacon. Put in the sliced chicken, and fry for ten minutes, then add some chicken stock or water, season with salt and paprika, and boil until the chicken is tender. Some sliced hard-boiled eggs can be added to it, and even pieces of lettuce as well.

The difference and the fun is in the paste with which you cover your so-called Arab pie. It is a very thin pastry, like our puff pastry, and the top looks like piecrust. Once I had the luck to see how this paste was made. I was just roaming about in Marrakesh when I saw an Arab woman make it while sitting on the ground in a yard.

She had a red-hot charcoal fire, and over this she put a good-sized copper bowl upside down. Meanwhile she mixed the paste with flour, a drop of oil, one egg, a little water, and salt—plenty of salt is needed to make it stretch. She worked it out very well, and then, holding it with one hand, stretched it with the other, until it was like a paper-thin sheet. When the copper bowl was fairly hot she placed one of the sheets on it, removing it when it was dry and not cooked too much. As each sheet was dry she took it off the bowl and put on another.

The pastilla is made up as we make our strudel. One sheet is put over the pie-dish and oiled well, and then another sheet is placed over it; more oil, another sheet, and so on, putting on five or six sheets and oiling each one before putting on the next. Before serving a little caster sugar is sprinkled on the top—and, of course, you must eat the dish with your fingers.

Turkey is the most decorative bird for a special occasion or for any buffet. Stuffed and roast, glazed with aspic (see page 26) and decorated, it really is a picture.

Stuffed Turkey
To make the stuffing chop the liver of the *Turkey*, mix it with minced pork, and fry with a little onion. Then mix with two or three whole eggs, a little cream, a little black pepper, and plenty of salt. Soak a very little white bread in milk, and mix with the stuffing.

There are, of course, many variations on this theme. Often I stuff the turkey with chestnut stuffing, which I make by boiling and skinning the chestnuts, then passing them through a sieve and mixing the purée with the other stuffing.

When stuffing the bird I always press the stuffing out to the breast, because it gives the meat a very good flavour. Then I sew it together, and season the turkey well with salt and paprika, really rubbing them in. All that remains now is to cover the turkey with lard or chicken fat and roast for three or four hours, according to the size of the bird.

Roast Turkey

I only roast a whole turkey for special occasions. When I have a turkey for our home use I commit a crime against the culinary law in this country. I cut the turkey in pieces!

I leave the breast and the upper parts of the wings in one piece, and stuff the breast in the same way as I would stuff a whole turkey. Then I roast it in the same way, first seasoning with salt and paprika and covering with lard or other fat. When it comes to the table nobody ever notices that it is not a whole turkey.

Roast Turkey
Legs

From the giblets and the back part of the turkey I make a soup. I salt and pepper the large legs, and put in a dish in the oven with carrots, celery, one shallot, one leek, one small onion, a clove of garlic, and some fat. First I roast the turkey legs on both sides, then I pour on a little chicken or veal stock and cover. When the meat is tender I take off the lid and let it get brown and crisp. Lastly I take out the vegetables and pass them through a sieve. With this dish you can, if you like, pour a little wine or cream in the gravy, and then you have an excellent and completely different roast. You can serve it hot or cold—either way it is good.

Turkey with
Oyster Sauce

Once in a private house in America I was given a superb dish of *Turkey Breast with Oyster Sauce*. The piece of turkey was shaped like a cutlet and even had a false bone in it. Each portion was salted and black-peppered and sautéed in butter till very tender. The pieces were beautifully served on a round silver dish, overlapping one another with asparagus-tips arranged round them. Very tiny new potatoes and French beans were served on a separate dish. Then there was the oyster sauce, and if you want to try this dish here is how to make it. Boil the oysters in salted water, then take them out of their shells and put them back in the liquid they were cooked in. Reduce this liquid, then add a little stock. Make a roux with a little butter and a little flour or potato flour, stirring till well blended, and add this to the liquid with the oysters while it is still cooking. Stir constantly, allow to boil for a few minutes, then season and add plenty of chopped parsley or chopped dill.

If the terrible thing happens to you that several of your farmer friends send you turkeys, and you are sick of the sight and taste of them, may I suggest a way of dealing with them that I think you and your family will like?

Smoked   Put some water in a big earthenware jar, and put in
Turkey   quite a lot of salt and very little saltpetre. Clean the turkey, inside and outside, and salt it well, rubbing the salt in. Make a few holes in the turkey meat with a pointed knife, and then put the turkey in the water, which should be just enough to cover it. Leave for three or four days, according to the size of the turkey. Then take it out, dry it with a cloth, and give it to a butcher who will send it to be smoked for three or four days. When you get it back you should hang it in a cold place and it will keep for weeks and weeks. When you want to use it you can boil the whole turkey or part of it. It is an excellent cold dish, similar to ham but much better.

Goose   The famous pâté de foie gras, made with truffles, comes from Strasburg, as nearly everyone knows. Hardly anyone knows that in the old days it was made from the livers of Hungarian geese. Rearing geese was a very important industry, and we exported thousands of goose livers to Strasburg. Some of them came back as the most expensive foie gras. We at home preferred the goose-liver in its natural form—so long as it was a big one, for small livers were no good. Mostly we bought geese for their livers, except for the very young ones in the spring. For our Whitsun dinner we always had young geese, and my father used to eat a whole one by himself. The young goose was just cleaned very well, seasoned with salt and paprika inside and outside, and roasted until crisp and brown-coloured. Fresh garden peas, cucumber salad, and new

potatoes were served with it. Doesn't it sound lovely?
It was.

We reared the fully grown geese ourselves for the
livers, and that meant we had to stuff them. This was the
cruellest thing on earth—happily it is not allowed in this
country. I still remember seeing a girl take two poor geese,
sit on them, and literally force food down their throats.
The food was maize that had been soaked in water with fat
added to it, and they were made to eat this three times a
day for five or six weeks. They hated it—a goose that had
once been forcibly fed would never eat voluntarily again.
They also had to drink salt water, and once during the
process a small brass coin—about the size of an English
farthing—was pushed down their throats. It was said that
this made the liver grow enormously, often by two or three
pounds.

Apart from the liver, we used these geese in many ways.
First of all we took off the very fatty skin, cut it in small
pieces, and made from it crackling, which was mostly eaten
cold. This was a great favourite with everybody. Then we
opened the goose, cleaned it inside, and removed the feet,
wings, and neck, and also the stomach after it had been
cleaned out. We cut the giblets in small pieces and either
made soup from them or used them for a risotto.

Goose Risotto

The risotto begins like a goulash. Chop one or two
onions finely, and fry until golden-brown, then add a good
teaspoon of paprika and one or two tomatoes—in winter
use tomato purée. Put in the small pieces of goose giblet,
and fry for a few minutes. Then pour on water or stock,
cook until the meat is tender but not quite ready, and add
one or two cupfuls of well-washed rice. You can also add
one chopped pimento, a few sultanas, one or two almonds,
and very little saffron. Boil until the rice is ready, and
serve with Parmesan cheese on top and tomato sauce.

Giblet Soup

When we made a soup from the goose giblets we garnished it with barley or noodles and served the giblets
separately with garlic sauce. For this we made a roux

C.F.L.—G

with a little goose fat and flour, which we cooked for only a few minutes so that it was still white; we poured some of the soup on this, then pressed two or three cloves of garlic through a presser and added them to the sauce. It was seasoned with salt and black pepper, and finally sprinkled with chopped parsley, and poured on the giblets. Garlic sauce is delicious if you can stand it. You can, of course, make a goulash or white-sauce dish out of the giblets instead.

Next we cut up the goose. First we took off the legs, cutting big, nice-looking pieces, and roasted them. To do this, leave on the fatty skin and add a little onion, a piece of garlic, a tomato, one or two mushrooms, a carrot, and a piece of celeriac and celery; roast until tender. If it is an oldish goose you can add a little water from time to time, and roast under cover; then, before it is quite ready, take off the cover and roast until nice and brown.

Breast of Goose   The breast of the goose is the best part, of course. This you can either roast or—as we often did—take the breast bone and mince it. Mix the minced meat with a piece of bread soaked in milk and one or two beaten eggs— it depends how much meat you have—season with salt and black pepper, and put back on the bone in its original shape. Then roast this in the same way as the legs. As children we loved it, and there was always the big question of who would get the bone, which had the best flavour of all.

Smoked Goose   Because geese were reared for their livers in Hungary, goose meat and goose fat could be bought quite cheaply. When there was too much of it we used to have it smoked. As for smoked turkey (see page 78), we had first to pickle the meat, and the process was much the same. We put plenty of salt and a little saltpetre in a jar, with an onion, a clove of garlic, a bayleaf and a few peppercorns. Then we stirred in the breast of the goose and the big legs, and kept the jar in a cold place for three or four days, turning the meat every day. Finally we took it out, dried it with a cloth, and sent it away to be smoked.

This smoked goose meat is very good cut in thin slices and eaten raw, like raw ham. Alternatively it can be stewed with sliced onions and paprika. Served with mashed potatoes, this makes a delicious meal. Like smoked turkey, when hung up in a cold larder smoked goose will keep for weeks and weeks.

Duck is a wonderful bird, but unluckily my grandfather spoiled it for me because he did not feel too kindly towards this nice friendly creature. He always used to say that ducks did not care what they ate, and as he cared perhaps more than enough what he ate he did not like them. He said they were not decent birds because they were not choosy about their food. But I think even he might have had a good word for wonderful Aylesbury ducks. *Duck*

This is what I usually do with duck. Take out all the giblets, and, if it is not very big, leave the bird whole. Cut the skin in squares without removing it from the duck but so that all the fat comes out. Rub in plenty of salt and paprika, then put it in a baking dish with a little goose or pork fat, one tomato, one clove of garlic, a piece of onion, the usual vegetables, and a sprig of marjoram. Braise it under cover until it is tender enough, then take off the cover and roast it until nice and crisp. Serve it with red cabbage, apple purée, redcurrant jelly, and new potatoes. *Roast Duck (Three Recipes)*

In Sweden once, in a private house, I had a delicious dish of roast duck stuffed with apples and prunes. It looked lovely—brown and crisp and well seasoned. It had obviously been rubbed inside and outside with salt and pepper, but this did not explain how the perfect colour and crispness had been achieved. I asked my hostess the secret. She told me that the duck had been basted very frequently, and when it was nearly ready it was basted with two or three tablespoons of cold water. Doing this, as I found myself when I tried it, makes the skin wonderfully crisp and brittle. It is important to leave the oven door slightly open to allow the steam to escape. *II*

The last time I was in Paris I had an excellent duck dish. *III*

It was a young duckling, with not much meat on it—that is really the trouble with young ducklings—but what there was of it was very good. It was roasted beautifully, brown and crisp, and served with an exquisite *Fig Sauce*. Of course I took the recipe and tried it out myself when I got home, and here is how it's made.

Take some fresh young green figs, and cook them in white wine. Add the gravy in which the duck has been roasted; if you haven't enough gravy, make up with brown stock. Boil up together, and take the fat off the top. Continue cooking for another ten minutes, then pour the sauce over the duck.

Serve the duck with young carrots, sautéd in butter with salt, and a little sugar, and sprinkled with chopped parsley, and with very small onions, also sautéd in butter.

CHAPTER SIX

THE GAME BAG

HUNGARY was so rich in all kinds of food that it used to be called the Granary of Europe. It was especially rich in game, ground and birds.

Game was so plentiful during the season that nobody had to go without it. You could buy it very cheaply. The cheapest and most popular was the hare, which was my father's favourite game after deer. My father was a very good shot and often brought home a whole deer and very many hares. Then not only did we have game in our house, but all our friends had the same for days and days.

When I think of game I recall old forgotten dinner parties, forgotten great occasions—engagement parties and weddings, with many relations and friends. I often wonder whether those people were really so much nicer than we are now—or is it only the great distance that makes it seem so? I think the same about the long-forgotten dishes with the wonderful flavours that can never quite be recaptured; or so it seems to me.

I can see us in our country home now, in the summer, when many relatives and friends came and stayed. I can hear the men deep in conversation—about politics, of course—praising or, more commonly criticizing the Government and the politicians of the day. Then my grandfather would interrupt all my uncles and cousins, saying, "Oh, my poor friends, you never knew the good old days—things were so much better then." At this there was always a heated argument, and then my grandmother stepped in and quietened poor old Grandpa, who never dared to disobey her.

While the men talked politics, the women sat together and discussed household troubles and especially cooking, and then they would exchange new recipes and busily write them into their already huge recipe books.

The paper is quite yellow now, and the ink is faded—but the recipes are still legible in those old books of my mother's, and of her mother's, and even of my grandmother's mother. For these recipe books have been kept with reverence and loving care, as if they were family heirlooms or old family lace. Sometimes in this changed world they are more valuable than either.

In England now, as in Hungary then, there is a big variety of game—not so cheap, of course, but then what is? And the old recipes are still as good—well, nearly as good—as they ever were.

Saddle of Venison   I like *Saddle of Venison*, one of the best parts of the deer. But you must make sure it is tender and juicy. First clean it, and, as far as possible, take out all the sinews. Then, with a larding needle, push in two or three rolls of fat bacon. After this prepare the brine, or, as it is sometimes called, the marinade. Take a large earthenware dish or jar, put in it three or four cleaned carrots, two to four small onions, sliced shallots, five or six black peppercorns, a few juniper seeds, parsley, and, if you care for it, thyme, one or two bay leaves, one clove of garlic, salt, a bottle of good white wine and a small glass of wine vinegar. Put your meat in this liquid, and leave it for twenty-four to thirty-six hours in a cold place.

When you take the meat out of the marinade, dry it with a cloth and then brush it all over with best-quality olive oil. Take a baking dish, put in some lard, and then put in your saddle of venison. Roast for a few minutes, then baste with a little of the marinade and roast in a medium oven until tender. (You can reckon twenty-five minutes for each pound of meat.) When it is tender and ready, take it out of the dish. Then put all the rest of the marinade in the baking dish, and let it boil until all the vegetables are tender. Taste for enough salt and add a little black pepper. Reduce it, then pass through a sieve. Add half a pint of fresh thick cream, heat up, and serve. This sauce should be served separately from the meat, which should be put in a long serving dish and garnished with boiled chestnuts, slices of cooked apples, or rings of pineapple. As vegetables serve red cabbage and boiled rice.

I do not marinate *Venison Cutlets*, but season them with salt and pepper and roast under cover with lard, basting with meat stock or red wine. When tender, make a *Sauce Romain*, as follows: caramelise two to four tablespoons of sugar, let it brown until a chocolate colour, then pour on it a few tablespoons of water until it dissolves. Put it aside. Remove the meat from the liquid in which it was roasted. Take off all the fat from this liquid, and add to it the dissolved browned sugar and half a pint of thick (if possible, sour) cream. Mix well. Season with salt and pepper. If the cream is not sour, add as much lemon juice as you like. Serve with mashed potatoes and redcurrant jelly.

Venison Cutlets Sauce Romain

For what I call *Hungarian Venison*, you need the bony part of the deer.

Hungarian Venison

Chop two or three large onions into some lard, add salt to taste, and sauté until golden brown. Add a good tablespoon of paprika, and small pieces of venison; sauté for a few more minutes before adding cold water or chicken stock. When tender, add plenty of fresh cream.

For *Venison Vanderbilt* you need a leg of deer. Roast it until it is not quite done, then let it cool, score deeply several times, and in each groove spread goose-liver paste (which you can buy in tins.) Close it into shape, and roast until tender. Baste with Madeira wine. Serve with small pieces of toast spread with goose-liver, and put a piece of truffle on each piece of toast.

Venison Vanderbilt

In Hungary we had so many hares when in season that we were always having to find new ways to cook them. I found the following recipe in a very old hand-written cookery book—God knows which of my grandmothers' or aunts' recipe it was!—and I remember our old cook making the dish. I have done it myself in this country, probably not half as well, but everyone seemed to like it a good deal.

Baked Hare   First catch your hare . . . the hare ought to be freshly shot, because the blood is needed for the cooking. Skin it, cut it up, and remove the inside. Put the heart, lungs, and liver aside in a bowl. Line a baking tin or fireproof dish with thin slices of smoked bacon and slices of onions, carrots, a piece of celeriac, a shallot, and a clove of garlic cut very small or smashed. Season the hare with salt and black pepper, and put it in the dish with dots of lard on it. Put in a hot oven, and brown on both sides. Then pour on four to five glasses of good red wine and the juice of one lemon, put on the lid, and simmer for one and a half to two hours.

Meanwhile mince the liver, heart, and lungs, and mix well with small chopped onions, a clove of garlic pressed through a garlic presser, salt and pepper, and some fresh cream. If you have been able to keep the hare's blood, add this to the sauce slowly, stirring all the time, and just simmer very carefully for fifteen minutes. (If you haven't the blood and need more liquid, add brown stock instead.)

When the hare is tender, take it out. Pass the liquid and vegetables through a sieve, mix with the purée of liver, heart, and lungs until it becomes a very creamy sauce, and put the hare back and bring to the boil. Put the hare on a long serving dish, and cover with this excellent sauce. Serve with roasted dumplings made with bread-cubes (see page 144).

Roast Hare   Here is another of our favourite ways of cooking hare. You need a nice large and young one if you can get it. Take the saddle off the hare, and lard it with a larding needle, using strips of lard or bacon. Put this saddle and the other part of the hare in an earthenware jar, and pour on it white wine and lemon slices. Add black peppercorns, salt, and a bay leaf, and let it marinate for two days. Take the hare out of the liquid, and roast with lard, browning each piece on all sides. Add the marinated liquid, and let it simmer until the hare is tender. Then take it out of the liquid, cut the saddle in pieces, and arrange it on a nice serving dish, and cover with a little of the sauce. Garnish with rice, stuffed tomatoes, and mushrooms. Serve the remaining sauce separately. If the sauce is too thin, add rich thick cream.

Pheasant

You cannot improve on cooking a young pheasant just plain, salted inside and out. Cover with thinly sliced bacon, put it in a baking tin with a small piece of butter or lard. Place it in the oven with one carrot, one leek and one piece of celery. Roast the pheasant first on both sides until brown and then baste with chicken or veal stock till tender. Before it is quite finished pour on it a few (four or five) tablespoons of fresh cream and, if you like, half a glass of red wine. Serve with game potatoes and cranberry sauce.

Pheasant à la Gipsy

For *Pheasant à la Gipsy* you need a bird that has been hanging for three or four days. Clean it, and stew in butter, with veal stock, tomatoes, small onions, chopped pimento, and salt. Baste with red wine.

Pheasant Sauté with Cream

If the pheasants are not as young as you would like them to be, this is a good way to cook them. Pluck, wash and clean them and salt well inside and out. Put in a casserole with a good piece of butter and a carrot sliced in long pieces and a celeriac sliced in the same way, and also a few shallots, six or eight pieces of mushroom and two tomatoes. Cook the bird and the vegetables until they are brown, then baste from time to time with sweet cream; carry on until the pheasant is tender. Then take out the bird from the casserole and pass all the vegetables through a sieve. Mix with a little more cream, taste for seasoning and then cut the pheasant in pieces just as you would a chicken. Place them in a long dish, pour the sauce over it and serve with flaky mashed potatoes, lentils and red-currant jelly.

Roast Partridge

Partridge has to be hung for a few days—to my taste not more than three, or at the most four, although I know some gourmets like it when it is high. After hanging, clean the bird and wash it well, salt inside and outside, sprinkle on a little flour, and roast in a baking tin with lard until nice and brown. In the meantime sauté half a pound or more mushrooms in butter, and add to the partridge. Pour on a few tablespoons of red wine, and simmer until tender. Cut the partridge in two, put the mushrooms on top, and pour on the sauce. Allow half a partridge per head. Serve with game potatoes and lentils.

Partridge with Lemon Sauce
    Another way to prepare partridge is with lemon sauce. Place the clean and washed partridge in a dish lined with slices of bacon, add a little stock, onions, carrots, parsnips, a few black peppercorns, a little sugar, salt, and put pieces of lard on the top. Put the lid on the dish and let it simmer, adding from time to time one or two tablespoons of meat stock. When the partridge is tender take it out. Reduce the liquid until it thickens, skim off the fat, and pass the liquid and vegetables through a sieve and add the juice and the grated peel of half a lemon, and bring to the boil again. Cut the partridge in four pieces, put it back into the sauce, and let it boil once more. Serve with slices of lemon and boiled rice.

Another Partridge Roast
    At a small, unpretentious restaurant in Paris I once had a delicious partridge with apples. A plump partridge was very well seasoned, roasted in butter and then cooked in stock until tender. It was cut in half and each portion was served on a piece of bread that had been sautéd in butter and then spread with a paste made by creaming the cooked liver of the partridge with a small amount of foie gras. The partridge and bread were put in a round dish, and the liquid the partridge had been cooked in was poured on it with the addition of some brandy. When it was brought to our table the brandy was set aflame, and the dish shaken until the flames were extinguished. The partridge was served with half-apples baked in butter, and it was a perfect dish.

Partridge Catalan
    Another good way of cooking partridge is the Catalan style. Sauté the partridge until tender, and blend its gravy

with concentrated tomato purée. Add to this sauce some pressed garlic cloves, lemon peel, and diced truffles. Strain the sauce, and add the partridge cut into pieces. Simmer for a few minutes.

For a change we sometimes have partridge served cold. *Cold Stuffed* Stuff the bird with a little truffled foie gras, then sew up *Partridge* the opening and cook until it is tender in butter and Madeira wine. Add salt and black pepper for seasoning. When cooked, let it cool, and then take the bird out of the sauce. Remove the fat from the sauce, add a little aspic (see page 26), and pour over the partridge when the bird is cold. Cold stuffed partridge looks magnificent when served on a silver dish decorated with pieces of foie gras and finely chopped aspic and with some radishes and green salad to brighten it up.

Grouse Bacchus is a good way of cooking this bird. Let *Grouse* it hang for three to four days, then clean, salt and roast in *Bacchus* butter, basting with white wine. Put raisins in the sauce, and pour in very thick cream before finishing.

For teetotallers grouse can just be roasted in butter. Add chopped green pimentoes and sour cream before serving.

I am afraid I am not a great friend of *Quails*, but some *Quails* gourmets are—mostly, I think, because they are very rare, especially now in this country. For those who appreciate this tiny bird I will describe how I ate it once in a French restaurant, for I very much liked the clever way it was served and garnished. The quails were just roasted in the usual way—browned in butter in a pan—and a little Madeira wine was added to the sauce. Then for each quail one artichoke heart was cooked in butter. A quail was placed on each artichoke heart; and chestnut purée, cooked and prepared as a savoury, was piped round it. The dish was covered with the sauce in which the quails were cooked, and it really looked like a nest with the bird in it. It was served on a round silver dish and decorated with some horse-radish and watercress.

CHAPTER SEVEN

BEGINNINGS, MIDDLES, AND ENDS

THE English language is full of pitfalls, and after talking little else for over a quarter of a century it still baffles me sometimes. I have never understood, for example, the meaning of the word "offal". I always thought it was stuff one put in the dustbin. My dictionary—the *Concise Oxford* —confirms this view. "Refuse, waste stuff, scraps, garbage", it calls it; "carrion, putrid flesh; offscourings, dregs"—and more in the same vein, with the compilers of the dictionary apparently working themselves up to a fine old rage. Yet when meat was rationed, Members of Parliament used this same abusive term for great delicacies like calf's liver, sweetbreads, and ox tongue. I was greatly puzzled—but perhaps that was because I do not understand politics either.

Pig's offal, as I suppose the politicians would call it, I have already talked about in the chapter on meat (see pages 50–67).

During and just after the war ox tongue was a great treat because, like other kinds of "offal", it was off the ration. As you remember, it was just a matter of getting it! When I was lucky enough to have one I always invited a few friends to enjoy it with us. It was not a novelty for us, for we often had it in the old days back home. (I love that American expression.) We pickled it and smoked it or just boiled it and ate it cold. For pickling we used salt, black pepper, a bay leaf, a clove of garlic, and an onion: we boiled all these up, then put in the tongue and left it for two to four days.

90

An *Ox Tongue* usually weighs five or six pounds—what a thing to carry all the time in your mouth! Here is one way of preparing it as a hot dish. First blanch the tongue by boiling it for an hour, and then remove the very rough skin. Sauté six very small onions, one clove of garlic, one carrot, one celeriac, and one small parsnip, until they are a nice golden-yellow. Put the tongue in a baking tin, and pour the sautéd vegetables over it. Add a pint of beef stock, and put in a not-too-hot oven. When it has cooked for an hour, add half a pint of red wine; go on cooking until the tongue is tender. Skim off the fat and strain the sauce, then put the tongue back in the oven and pour on it another glass of good red wine. Mix two tablespoons of flour in half a pint of cream, and pour this on the tongue. Let it boil for only a few minutes more, then serve with creamy mashed potatoes and fresh green peas.

Ox Tongue (Hot)

Another of my favourite ways of doing *Ox Tongue* is *with an Onion Mousse*. To make this, grate four large onions, season with salt and black pepper, and mix with cream and two or three egg-yolks. Get a large ox tongue —and, again, first blanch it by boiling in water, this time with salt, a bay leaf, and a few black peppercorns. Simmer until you can take the skin off easily. Then cut the tongue lengthways in half, and spread both cut sides with onion mousse. Put the two pieces together with a skewer, so that the onion mousse is like the filling in a sandwich, then cover the whole of the tongue with onion mousse. Put in a baking-tin with some lard, and finish in the oven until tender.

Ox Tongue with Onion Mousse

From the tongue to the tail—to a very old Hungarian peasant dish made with *Ox-Tail*, which I pass on because it really is good. Ask the butcher to cut the ox-tail in pieces, and at the same time get two pig's feet and, if you can, half a pig's head; these should also be cut in pieces when you buy them. Remove the unnecessary bones, and put the rest into cold water. Add salt, paprika, a few black peppercorns, one onion, and one clove of garlic. Boil for

Ox-Tail (Hungarian)

hours, according to size, skimming from time to time. When the meat is nearly soft enough, add all the vegetables you can put your hands on—carrots, parsnips, celery, celeriac, half a cabbage, four or five tomatoes, and leeks. When all the vegetables are tender, skim very carefully, taking off all the fat, add chopped parsley, and serve in a big soup tureen. It has to be eaten from soup plates and should be served with boiled potatoes. Remember that there is not much meat in an ox-tail, so buy as many as you are likely to need.

Kidneys (Ox) in White Wine

Ox Kidneys are cheap and pleasant if they are cooked long enough to be tender; and very tasty when done with *White Wine*. Blanch the kidneys for a few minutes in hot water, then remove the skin and fat. Sauté them whole in hot lard, season with salt and pepper, add beef stock and simmer till tender. Add half a pint of white wine, then boil until the sauce thickens. Serve with new potatoes generously sprinkled with chopped parsley and butter.

Kidneys in Madeira

Calf's and sheep's kidneys do not need so much cooking, and both are delicious with Madeira sauce. First clean the kidneys, removing the fat and skin, and then cut them in thin slices. Season with salt. Put some lard in a frying pan, and when it is very hot put in the kidneys. Stir. Meanwhile slice some mushrooms, season and sauté them, and add these to kidneys in the frying pan. Pour on a little veal or chicken stock, and when the kidneys are tender, pour over them some Madeira sauce. To make this you simply put three tablespoons of good Madeira wine in a saucepan, add about ten tablespoons of good brown stock, and boil for fifteen minutes. Serve with chopped parsley sprinkled over the dish.

Kidneys (Pig) in White Wine

One of the best kidney dishes I ever tasted was made with *Pig's Kidneys*, and I came across it in France. Slice the kidneys fairly thinly, and season well with salt and black pepper, then sauté in butter with sliced onions. Sprinkle potato flour on the kidneys while they are frying —it makes the sauce smooth and thick. Then pour some good white wine over the kidneys and cook till tender. Sauté button mushrooms separately, and mix together with the kidneys. Serve with savoury rice.

I have talked about what we used to do with the pig's head, making pork cheese or brawn (see page 64). A calf's head can also be made into a number of good dishes. It can, for example, be used for a hot-pot, with lots of vegetables; or you can make a soup out of it; or you can do it in jelly, and this is one of the best ways of all.

Calf's Head in Jelly

Cut the head in four to six pieces—better, let your butcher do it for you!—and leave in the tongue but take out the brain. (Another good dish can be made from that, and I shall describe it as soon as I have finished with the calf's head jelly.) Put the pieces of head and tongue in cold water with a clove of garlic, one onion, one leek, two carrots, one parsnip, a piece of celery, celeriac, two or three tomatoes, a few peppercorns, and salt. Boil slowly with just enough water to cover it properly. When nearly tender, add two egg-whites to clarify the liquid. Take off the scum. Remove the meat and the nice pieces of vegetables—not the onion or garlic, of course—and arrange first the vegetables and then the meat pieces in a dish. Skin the tongue and then cut it in pieces, and arrange them nicely with the meat. Take all the fat off the liquid, sieve through a cloth, and pour over the meat. Let it cool. Put the dish in the refrigerator. Decorate with hard-boiled eggs and sliced tomatoes and watercress, and serve with horse-radish sauce (see page 122).

Calf's Brains on Pumpernickel

There are several ways of using the calf's brains. One is stewing them and spreading them on buttered Pumpernickel. The brains should first be boiled in salt water for five minutes, after the skin is removed, stewed with some sautéd onions or chives, and finally pressed through a sieve. Now take a slice of Pumpernickel, turn both sides in hot butter, and spread the calf's brain on it.

Calf's Brains with Cheese Sauce

Calf's brains go well also with a cheese sauce. First poach the brains in beef stock, seasoned with salt and black pepper. Take out after a few minutes, and remove all the skin. Then put the brains in a buttered fireproof dish. Make a white sauce with a little butter and flour and a little milk, and add grated Parmesan or Gruyère cheese. Mix very gently; if you work too hard with the cheese it will become leathery. Pour the sauce over the brains, and cook in the oven or under the grill for about ten minutes. Sprinkle with chopped parsley.

Calfs' sweetbreads also can be done in many ways. First of all always wash and clean the sweetbreads and soak them in cold water until all traces of the blood have disappeared. Then blanch the sweetbreads, putting them in cold water and letting them come to the boil, then taking them out and putting them into cold water—and, of course, removing whatever skin you can.

Sweetbread Sauté

When the sweetbreads are blanched you can cut them in thin strips, sauté a little onion and a little celery, and add these to the sweetbreads, with salt and black pepper, and then sauté all together till well cooked. Serve with Béchamel sauce (see page 117).

Sweetbread Vol-au-Vent

Another way is to sauté some mushrooms with an onion, add a little paprika, and pour on some fresh cream; mix with the blanched sweetbreads, and cook till they are done. You can use this as a *vol-au-vent* filling or you can serve them on buttered toast; or you can make a white-wine sauce (see page 184) and serve with rice.

Chilled Sweetbread

In a private house in America I had *Chilled Sweetbreads* as a first course. Wash, soak, and blanch the sweetbreads as usual, and cut them in long slices. Cut some shallots in pieces and sauté them in butter for a few minutes; add some button mushrooms and cook for a few minutes more, then add the sliced sweetbreads. Sprinkle with a little potato flour or rice flour, stir, add salt and black pepper and a little veal stock, and boil till it thickens, then add cream and egg-yolks. Allow to cool. Make long-shaped croquettes from the sweetbreads when they are cold, rolling them first in a mixture of egg and a little milk and

then in ground almonds. Fry in hot chicken fat or oil.
Allow to cool and chill, and serve with ice-cold tomato
sauce (see page 121) and salad.

When you buy calf's liver make sure that it is very *Liver*
young. (It should be very light in colour.) Take off the
skin if you can without spoiling the liver, then put it in
milk for a few hours—this will give it a lighter colour.
Sauté some very finely cut onions in chicken fat, add the
liver cut in thin slices, and about a teaspoon of paprika. It
should not need more than ten to fifteen minutes. Serve
as soon as it is done with new potatoes or a really good
savoury rice (see page 139).

As I have hundreds and hundreds of chickens, since I
need to supply my own restaurant and catering department
daily with fresh eggs and roasting chickens, I always have
a lot of chicken liver. There are many ways of cooking it,
and one of my favourites is frying the liver with onions
and then making a risotto of it with mushrooms and fresh
peas and rice. But now I have found a new way, and as it
has been voted a success I shall give you the recipe. It is a
Chicken Liver Purée with Lobster Sauce.   *Chicken Liver*
Purée with
Take one pound of fresh chicken liver and pass it   *Lobster Sauce*
through a wire sieve. Mix thoroughly with some butter,
already well creamed, and three whole eggs and three or
four extra egg-yolks. Work well together, and season
with salt—of which liver needs a lot—and red and black
pepper: it is best if you grind the black pepper freshly,
add some cream. Mix well; it should be rather soft, not
firm. Butter a fireproof dish, pour in the mixture, and let
it cook in steam for two hours on a very low flame. When
it is ready, turn it out into a glass dish.

While the chicken liver purée is steaming, make the
very interesting sauce. First make a very little white sauce
with butter and flour, slowly adding milk and letting it
boil for a few minutes. Take this off the heat, and add to it
a good half-pint of Jersey cream, salt and pepper, and a
tablespoon of good brandy. (When you use brandy, always

C.F.L.—H

use a good one—and don't forget to flame it to get rid of
the spirit flavour.) Add one tablespoon of lobster butter
or crab butter (see page 44). Mix well. When the sauce
is to your taste, cut the meat from one boiled crab or lobster into small pieces, and add to the sauce. Mix well and
put back on the fire for a few minutes. Let it simmer, but
don't let it boil. Pour the sauce over the chicken liver
purée, spread freshly chopped parsley on the top, and
serve with rice. This is good as a first course or main dish.

Tripe　　If I want to cheer my husband up I make one of his
favourite dishes. Fortunately he has many favourites,
including one very unlikely delicacy—tripe! Not with
onions, though. My husband says there is only one way to
do tripe, and that is with garlic.

It is at least easy to cook tripe in this country, because
it is cleaned so beautifully. In Hungary we had to clean it
for quite a while, and then we had to let it soak for a few
hours in salted water: here it is all done for us.

I buy just a pound of tripe—my husband is the only one
in the house who likes it—cut it in long thin strips, and
boil for about half an hour in about a pint of salted water.
Then I make roux with lard and flour, and stir it for a
few minutes over the fire but do not let it brown. I press
a clove of garlic through the garlic presser and add this to
the roux together with a very little cold water; bring it to
the boil, simmer for a few minutes, and then add black
pepper and salt. Finally I put the roux in with the tripe—
still in the water it was boiled in—and boil for about
twenty minutes. I serve the tripe with a generous sprinkling of chopped parsley and with a bowl of boiled rice.

I have been very daring in trying out many Continental
dishes on my English friends, but I have never dreamed of
giving them this tripe dish. Perhaps I have been wrong.
So you try it—on your husbands. According to my own
feeling about it I think it must be a man's dish.

CHAPTER EIGHT

ALL KINDS OF
VEGETABLES

POTATOES are the delight of the poor and rich alike. All the year round, every day, almost at every meal, most people eat potatoes—and enjoy them. They are always welcome—and you never get tired of them because they can be cooked in hundreds and hundreds of ways. But I think they are delightful in their simplest and most obvious forms. What, for example, can be more appetising than snow-white plain boiled potatoes piled up on any dish? Or can you imagine anything nicer on a cold winter's evening than a well-baked potato in its jacket with a little good butter and salt?

Still, even with potatoes variety is never out of place, and there are several good potato dishes that are not at all widely known in this country. For example, there is what we as children called the *"King of Potatoes"*.

Boil six or eight large potatoes in their skins and hard-boil six eggs. When cooked, peel the potatoes, shell the eggs, and cut both in fairly thin, round slices. Generously butter an earthenware casserole. Place a layer of sliced potatoes on the bottom, then a layer of egg on top; sprinkle with salt and add a little cream—preferably sour cream. Repeat this until all the ingredients are used. You should finish with the top layer of potatoes. Pour a little more cream on this, and dot the top with butter. Altogether you should use about three-quarters of a pint of cream and a quarter of a pound of butter. Use another quarter of a pound of butter to roast white breadcrumbs in the oven until they are

King of Potatoes

golden-brown. Cover the dish with these roasted bread-crumbs, place it in a moderately hot oven for half an hour, and serve as a garnish or a first course.

Jacket   Potatoes boiled in their skins can be delicious when
Potatoes   mixed with a good sauce—a pleasant-flavoured tomato sauce, for example; garnished with fresh chopped parsley, you can serve them with any meat. Alternatively mix the potatoes with a sauce made from sour cream, peeling them first.

Potato   Typically Hungarian, of course, is *Potato Goulash*. Fry
Goulash (Two a large, finely chopped onion until it is golden-brown,
Recipes)   then add a teaspoon of paprika. Peel the potatoes, and cut each lengthwise into four pieces. Put them into a saucepan, stir in the onion for a minute, and add salt. (As you know, potatoes take quite a lot of salt.) Add one or two chopped tomatoes and, if available, green peppers. Cover with water and boil until tender. Add a few carraway seeds to taste.

II   Alternatively boil the potatoes in their skins, and mean-while sauté large finely chopped onions until golden-brown. Add a teaspoon of paprika to the onions. When the potatoes are boiled, skin them and cut them into round slices. Mix with the onions and fat, add salt, and serve immediately. This is the favourite potato dish in my house.

For many years my husband and I celebrated birthdays together with our oldest English friends. These very pleasant occasions were usually held in our house although sometimes in our friends' country cottage. Once on my husband's birthday I told them they would be having a Hungarian dish. I made it because it was one of his favourite potato dishes, and I told them they would have to put up with it. So they did—and whenever they came to us after that we had to have this so-called *Garlic Potato*. This is how I make it:

Garlic   Boil six or eight large potatoes in their skins. Don't
Potato   boil them too long, for they have to be boiled again in the sauce. Peel and cut into rounds. Make a white roux from an ounce and a half of lard and two tablespoons of flour.

Stir over the gas for a minute, then stir in one or two finely crushed cloves of garlic. Now add a pint and half of cold water, and season with salt and black pepper, then mix everything together and bring to the boil. Before serving add quite a lot of chopped parsley.

The Italians have an interesting potato dish. First boil *An Italian* the potatoes, then cut them into slices and place in a sauce- *Potato Dish* pan with a piece of butter, salt, and chopped parsley. Add one chopped onion, a teaspoon of flour, and a quarter of a glass of white wine. Cook for about ten minutes, and serve very hot.

Puff Potatoes always go down well. Peel good large *Puff* potatoes, and cut them evenly into thick slices. Dry the *Potatoes* slices in a tea-cloth, and put them in hot fat—but not too hot. Let them cook for about four or five minutes, stirring or moving them constantly. Take them out of the pan as soon as they rise to the surface and begin to puff up. Drain. Have ready another pan containing very hot fat, and drop the potatoes in for another second. They will puff up and be very crisp, and will stay crisp.

Potato Croquettes are another favourite. Boil the *Potato* potatoes in salted water, drain, and rub through a wire *Croquettes* sieve: use a lump of butter to work the purée to a creamy consistency. Stir in some egg-yolks, mix well, and form the mixture into small long rolls. Roll these lightly in flour. Mix one or two whole eggs together with a little salt, and dip the potato croquettes into this, then into breadcrumbs, and fry in hot fat just before serving. If you like you can mix some cooked garden peas with the potato purée.

Potatoes for game are made in the same way as the *(For Game)* croquettes, except that you add two ounces of stoneless raisins. Shape them like balls, roll in flour, roll in egg and then in breadcrumbs, and fry as above.

For an interesting way of doing potatoes that I came *A German* across in Germany, cut some potatoes very evenly, like *Potato Dish* matches, wash and wipe dry, and place in a frying pan with a quarter of a pound of melted butter. Add salt and black pepper. Roll the potatoes in the butter and let them brown on one side, then turn like a pancake and brown the other side. Serve very hot.

One more thing about potatoes—in case you don't know already: they contain plenty of Vitamins A and B, and a good deal of C and G—according to the wise books.

Of course, a lot of potatoes may not be a great help to anyone who is trying to reduce weight. However, if you are anxious to keep your schoolgirl or schoolboy figure—I really don't know whether women or men are slimming more nowadays, I hear so much about it from both—you can at least eat tomatoes to your heart's content. Large quantities are allowed even in the strictest slimming diet. And they are very health-giving whether you are slimming or not.

Tomato Salad Tomatoes are at their best if you take them from your own garden. I have some, and I even like them when they are flowering, as they are very pretty. When ripe they are lovely to look at, and good to eat in a variety of ways. Personally, though, I like them best raw in a salad. Just slice them thinly with a drop of lemon juice, some finely sliced onions, and chopped parsley or chopped chives.

Tomato and A very popular dish in Hungary was *Tomato and*
Pimento *Pimento*, which we called green or red paprika. Cut six large fresh tomatoes in slices, then cut three green pimentoes the same way—but be careful to take out all the pimento seeds and veins as they are very hot. Cook in butter until tender. Beat three eggs, add salt, and mix the whole together. Cook for only one or two more minutes, and serve very hot.

Stuffed Tomatoes are very good stuffed in the French way.
Tomatoes Mince a little cooked beef, veal, or ham. Chop some onions
(French) finely, and cook lightly in a little butter; add some chopped mushroom, and mix with the mincemeat. Add salt, pepper, and chopped parsley, and mix until smooth. Add one or two tablespoons of cream. Cut the tomatoes in half, if they are big—use them whole if they are small—scoop out the

middles, and fill with the mince mixture. Sprinkle with breadcrumbs and a little butter on the top. Place in a hot oven for ten or fifteen minutes, and serve as a first course or garnish.

Italian stuffed tomatoes are done in much the same way, but the stuffing is risotto. If you like, you can add grated cheese to the rice. When stuffed, sprinkle the tomatoes with chopped parsley, breadcrumbs, and oil or butter, and put in the oven to brown for fifteen to twenty minutes.

Stuffed Tomatoes (Italian)

Onions also are good stuffed. Use large round ones, scoop out the middles, and boil for ten minutes. Drain and stuff with chopped ham, chopped eggs, or chopped mushroom—whichever you use should already have been fried with chopped onions and then mixed with cream. Place the stuffed onions in a baking dish, and pour on it enough stock to half-cover them. Sprinkle with breadcrumbs that have been browned in butter, and serve very hot.

Stuffed Onions

The large Spanish onions are best for ordinary frying, and should be cut in big round slices. Separate the rings, salt well, and let them stand for twenty minutes. Now take them out of their liquid and put them in a dry clean tea-cloth. Put them in a dish of milk for a few minutes, take out and dry. Roll them in flour, then drop into very hot deep fat, and fry for four or five minutes. Drain. Reheat the fat, and drop the onions in a second time. Fry until golden-brown.

Fried Onions

Pimento, or paprika, is a distinctively Hungarian vegetable, and *Stuffed Pimento* or paprika is a Hungarian national dish. At least, we say it is, although there are other claimants. Yugoslavia says it is a Yugoslav national dish, the Bulgarians protest that it is theirs, and of course Turkey says it is and always was a purely Turkish dish. There is a standing discussion about it, but luckily it has not yet reached the breaking point in the diplomatic field. In this country I think I am probably safe from serious contradiction when I assert again that whatever anyone else says, it is definitely a Hungarian national dish.

Stuffed Pimento

Take eight to ten pimentoes, not too large; they can be red, green, or yellow. Clean out the insides very thoroughly, removing the unpleasantly hot seeds and veins. Put in salted hot water for ten or fifteen minutes. Boil half a pound of rice for a few minutes, and mix with it half a pound of minced pork and salt and black pepper. Chop a very small onion finely, and fry it in a little fat; then mix it with the pork and rice, pouring on half a cup of boiling water. Take the pimentoes out of the salted water, and stuff carefully with the mixture, until each pimento is full. Take a half-pound tin of concentrated tomato purée, and dilute it with hot water so that it is pleasantly thin but not watery, and add salt and sugar to taste. Cook the pimentoes in the tomato sauce for an hour and a half. Add a quarter of a pint of fresh cream, and serve with noodles, spaghetti, or potatoes.

Carrots   One of my favourite vegetables is the carrot, which is cheap and very good when young and old alike. Cut them if they are large, but if they are small cook them whole. Boil in salt water or in milk until tender, then drain and fry in salted butter. Cover with cream and chopped parsley, and serve.

(A Garnish)   As a garnish carrots are decorative and useful for your colour scheme. Cut some into small round shapes—or any other shape you may prefer—and place in a saucepan with enough chicken stock to cover, and season with salt, sugar, and a little pepper. Cover with a lid and boil very slowly until all the liquid has been absorbed and forms a thin jelly which covers the carrots. Sprinkle with chopped parsley.

Carrots à la   To make *Carrots à la St. Moritz*—and they are well
St. Moritz   worth making—slice one pound very finely, and place in a saucepan with a quarter of a pound of butter, salt, and a teaspoon of sugar, and cover with cold water. Put on a lid, and boil until the water has evaporated. Serve immediately with a lot of parsley.

Parsley is a wonderful herb, modest but very decorative. It stimulates the appetite, helps digestion, and I am

told that it is rejuvenating. It has a lot of vitamins A and
C and contains iron. Never be without it in your kitchen.
It is very easy to grow your own, and if you live in a flat
the tiniest window-box will do; buy the seeds in the spring,
plant in good soil, and let the sun do the rest. You will
always be sure of fresh parsley then.

Cabbage, like carrot, is cheap and good. Of the many
different ways of cooking it, to my mind, none can compare with stuffed cabbage, which is virtually a Hungarian
national dish. No festival, holiday, Sunday or other special
occasion was complete without stuffed cabbage on the table.

To prepare this dish you must first make some sauerkraut. You can, of course, buy this in shops, either from a
big barrel or in tins; but that is not the real thing. In any
case, sauerkraut is very simple to make at home from the
fresh cabbage that you can buy nearly the whole year
round—and it is so worth-while.

To make the *Sauerkraut*, then, take a large, hard cab- *Sauerkraut*
bage, and cut it in two. Remove the outside leaves if they
are too hard, but not otherwise; for these are the best part
of the cabbage, having been kissed by the sun. Wash the
cabbage, and remove the hard core. Then shred very finely
with a good sharp knife. Take a large glass or earthenware
jar, and pack it with the shredded cabbage until it is half
full. Add a few carraway seeds, a few black peppercorns,
and some dill, and then fill the jar with the rest of the
shredded cabbage. Add hot, but not too hot, water, with
some salt, until the jar is absolutely full. Cut a good slice
of bread, either brown or white, and place it on top of the
jar. Press it down until it is completely covered with
water. Keep it in a warm place for three days, near the
stove or, if possible, on a window-sill in warm sunshine. It
will then be pleasantly sour—like sour wine. Remove the
bread. There you have the sauerkraut.

Now take another large cabbage, and place it in boiling *Stuffed*
water for ten to fifteen minutes. Take off the outer leaves, *Cabbage*
being careful not to break them. From the leaves cut away (*Hungarian*)

the hard core. Then take half a pound of minced pork, half a pound of minced beef, and a quarter of a pound of well-washed rice. (It is a good thing to boil the rice for a few minutes in salted water.) Chop a small onion, and fry in a spoonful of fat until a golden colour. Mix together the meat, onions, and rice, and salt and black pepper. Stuff the cabbage leaves by putting a handful of the mixture into each leaf and then rolling it and sealing both ends so that the mixture does not come out.

Now take a large onion, slice finely, and fry it for a few minutes in a large saucepan in a quarter of a pound of lard. Add the shredded cabbage of the sauerkraut, and mix well with a spoonful of red pepper. Put in a piece of ham or pork, and put the stuffed cabbage-leaves on the top. Pour on the juice from the sauerkraut, and boil for two hours. Place on top three or four tomatoes or tomato purée.

Take two ounces of lard and three tablespoons of flour, and make a roux. Heat until golden-brown, and add a little paprika. Pour water on to the thickening. Take out the stuffed cabbage, and mix the thickening with the shredded sauerkraut and with the liquid in which the stuffed cabbage was boiled. Replace the stuffed cabbage. Before serving add half a pint of cream, sour or fresh.

This stuffed cabbage is supposed to taste much better after being warmed up. I have known families in Hungary who made their stuffed cabbage on Sunday and warmed it up every day, and they said that it was at its best on Saturday—when it had been reheated six times!

Stuffed Cabbage (French) The French stuff cabbage with chestnuts. Put a large cabbage in boiling water, and at the same time skin and boil sixteen French chestnuts. Fry some boiled ham, and cut it into small pieces. Take the half-cooked cabbage out of the water and cut out its heart, and in place of this put the boiled chestnuts. Tie the stuffed cabbage in a cloth, and braise in chicken stock for two hours. Drain, and cover with cream, fresh or sour. Sprinkle with Parmesan cheese, and serve with the pieces of ham surrounding the cabbage.

To cook *Green Cabbage*, wash and cut off the stalk and
the outer leaves, cook for half an hour in stock, and drain.
Then place strips of bacon at the bottom of a pan, and cover
with the cabbage. Season with salt and paprika. Add enough
stock to half-cover the cabbage, cover with a lid, and cook
until all the liquid has been absorbed. Before serving,
sprinkle with breadcrumbs that have been browned in a
little butter.

Green Cabbage

Cauliflower is, I think, best plain boiled in salt and
water, drained, and served with brown sauce or butter.
But it needs to be of perfect quality for this treatment; if
it is not snow-white, or not as good as it should be, then a
less simple recipe is required.

Cauliflower au Gratin is, in my opinion, best made with
Béchamel Sauce (see page 117) and two sorts of cheese.
First boil the cauliflower, and drain. Butter a fireproof dish,
put in a layer of cauliflower, and sprinkle with grated
Parmesan cheese. Pour on it two tablespoons of Béchamel
sauce. Add another layer of cauliflower, sprinkle with
grated Gruyère cheese, and add another two tablespoons
of Béchamel sauce. Continue in this way, alternating with
Parmesan and Gruyère cheese, until the dish is full.
Finally sprinkle melted butter on the top and brown it
under the grill.

Cauliflower au Gratin

Spinach is a very good and health-giving vegetable, and
naturally it has a high reputation in a vitamin-conscious
world. There are several good ways of doing it.

Spinach

Take three pounds of spinach—which is not a large
amount—wash it very thoroughly, and boil in very, very
little salted water for ten minutes. Drain it and pass it
through a sieve. Cook an ounce of flour in an ounce of
melted butter till golden-yellow. Add a quarter of a pint
of milk, and boil for a few minutes. Mix with the spinach,
and add salt, black pepper, and a soupçon of finely crushed
garlic. Pour on one or two egg-yolks mixed with a little
fresh cream, mix well, and serve.

For families with children I recommend slices of white bread, soaked in milk and a beaten egg and fried in hot fat, served on top of the spinach.

Spinach Soufflé

Spinach Soufflé makes a pleasant change. Again take three pounds of spinach, and cook in a very little salted water, drain and pass through a sieve. This time make the thickening with two ounces of butter and an ounce and a half of flour. It must stay white, so only cook it for two minutes, stirring all the time. Remove from the heat, and slowly add three beaten egg-yolks to the sauce. Add to the spinach. Whip the whites of the eggs very stiffly, and carefully mix with the spinach. Butter a fireproof soufflé dish, and pour in the whole of the mixture. Sprinkle generously on top with grated Parmesan cheese, and put in moderate oven for thirty to thirty-five minutes. Serve in the same dish, as a garnish or a first course.

Brussels Sprouts

Brussels Sprouts are another health-giving vegetable, rich in vitamins—but I cook them only if the kitchen is very far away from the living-rooms, as nobody wants to have the smell even if they like the taste. I like them best boiled in a very little salted water and served with browned butter. If only we could eliminate that smell!

Celery

Celery needs to be washed very thoroughly. One way of cooking it that I like is cutting the stalks in half lengthwise, boiling for fifteen to twenty minutes in salted water, and then braising for an hour in its own juice or in seasoned stock with slices of onion and carrot. Before serving, pour a glass of Madeira wine over it.

Celery (Italian)

A good alternative is the Italian way. Cook the celery in chicken stock, and drain well. Place in a baking dish with Mornay sauce (see page 119). Sprinkle with cheese, and brown in a hot oven.

Celeriac

Celeriac is one of my favourite vegetables, and it is worth taking the trouble to get it. I like it with Parmesan cheese. Use plenty of celeriac, clean it thoroughly, and allow to simmer until cooked; before serving, sprinkle with Parmesan cheese. I also like celeriac fried. Cut it into round slices, and cook it well in salted water; drain and allow to dry. Roll in flour, egg, and breadcrumbs. Fry in hot fat or oil, and serve with tomato sauce.

Broccoli is a very good decorative vegetable. I cook it in well-salted water, and, after draining it, pour on melted butter. *Broccoli*

Everyone can cook *Fresh Garden Peas*, and I do not think one can improve on the simple way. I just boil the young and freshly opened peas with a little salt water, drain, and add a little butter, a pinch of sugar, and chopped parsley. For a change, however, I sometimes cook them differently. Take two pounds of green peas and three ounces of butter, put in a pan and add a tablespoon of flour. Mix thoroughly. Add salt and sugar and twelve to eighteen very small onions and a finely sliced lettuce. Add just enough water to cover. Cook in a hot oven for twenty minutes. Before serving, sprinkle with a lot of chopped parsley, or with finely chopped mint. *Fresh Garden Peas*

Split Peas are a vegetable that are much liked and used in Germany and Eastern Europe, and also quite a lot in Hungary. Wash the dried peas, and soak in cold water overnight. Cook with just enough water to cover them. Add one onion, one clove of garlic, and a few slices of bacon, and cook over a small flame slowly for an hour. Pass through a sieve, and cook until thick. Before serving, cut the onion into long strips, fry it in hot fat until golden-brown, then add half a teaspoon of paprika and pour into the dish on top of the split peas. *Split Peas*

French Beans are best cooked in plenty of salt water, which keeps their green colour. Boil very quickly, and never cover with a lid. Serve with hot butter. Alternatively mix with a light Béchamel sauce (see page 117) and serve with chopped parsley. *French Beans*

We used to serve *Lentils* as vegetable with all kinds of game, venison, duck, grouse, hare, and so on. Clean and wash half a pound of lentils, boil in salted water, and add to the water a piece of lemon with the skin on, some small *Lentils*

firm onions, and one bay leaf. Boil the lentils until tender.
Make a roux with a tablespoon of lard and a good tablespoon of flour. Stir until a nice dark golden-brown, then
dilute with cold water. Boil it down if thin, and add sugar
and lemon according to taste. Drain the lentils and add the
roux. If you like you can pass the lentils through a sieve
and serve them as lentil purée.

Marrow   Vegetable *Marrow* is a modest vegetable with which I
(*My Style*) have had a lot of fun and quite a bit of success. Whenever
I serve it to guests in my home they never want to believe
that it is ordinary vegetable marrow. When I offer it to
my customers for dinner parties they all, without exception, say, "Oh, no, not marrow—it is an awful watery
tasteless thing." It takes all my persistence to persuade
them to let me prepare it for them to try once. I always
say, "Try it and taste it. If you don't like it we shan't serve
it, and I shall not charge for it." Once they have tasted it,
however, they order it again and again. It is a very good
vegetable for roast pork, roast duck, or goose. This is how
I do it.

The marrow should be of a good large size, and it must
be young and tender. To find out whether it is tender
enough try it with your finger-nail; if it goes in easily,
then it is young.

Peel the marrow and cut off both ends. Cut it in half
lengthwise and scoop out all the inside pips, and slice it to
the thickness of a match. There is a very clever slicing
machine which slices marrow on one side and cucumber on
the other. It would be more correct to say it shreds than
slices, and the marrow comes out looking like spaghetti.

When it is sliced, or shredded, salt it and let it stand in
the salt for five to ten minutes. Take a large saucepan, put
in a quarter of a pound of butter, allow it to melt, and put
the marrow in it. If it is very watery, press a little water
out gently with your hand. Put it in the butter immediately. Sprinkle two tablespoons of white vinegar on it,
otherwise it will mash in no time. Stir it, and sprinkle with

two tablespoons of white flour. Cook for ten minutes, and pour on a quarter of a pint of cream. Add a little sugar to taste. After boiling it with the cream for a few minutes on a slow flame, put in a good handful of chopped dill. Now put in the serving dish an egg-yolk beaten up with another quarter of a pint of cream. Mix well together, and pour the hot marrow on it. Again sprinkle the top with chopped dill.

For *Stuffed Marrow*, mix half a pound of minced pork with lightly fried chopped onions and very little black pepper. Cook half a cup of well-washed rice with half a cup of water for a few minutes only. Clean and chop two mushrooms and sauté in a little butter. Mix the meat and onions, rice, and mushrooms together, and put on one side. *Stuffed Marrow*

Peel a very young marrow, and cut off the stem end. Hollow the marrow carefully, to take out all the pips but not the flesh. Stuff in the mixture, after first having salted it well. When the marrow is well stuffed, put back the cut piece on the end. Now take a fireproof dish the size of the marrow, butter it well and put the marrow in it. Pour a quarter of a pint of cream on top, and cook it in an oven until tender. Serve with breadcrumbs that have been browned in butter.

There is a very small and young marrow called *Courgette*. It should not be bigger than a carrot. Wash and boil in salted water for a few minutes. Drain, and serve with hot melted butter. *Courgette*

The *Asparagus* with the best flavour in this country is the green-tipped variety called grass asparagus. It should be scraped and washed, tied in bundles, and cooked in salted water—very gently, otherwise the tips will fall off. Keep it warm in the salted water until serving. Serve on a napkin with fresh parsley and Hollandaise sauce (see page 121). *Asparagus (Three Recipes)*

Another way of preparing it is to arrange the cooked asparagus side by side so that the tips are visible, sprinkle *II* with grated Gruyère cheese, and pour over it a lot of brown butter; then place in a very hot oven for three minutes, and serve.

III   Asparagus tips can be combined in one dish with artichokes. Wash the artichokes thoroughly, cleaning the bottoms, and cook in butter in a covered pan over a low heat. Arrange in an oval dish, and surround with the asparagus tips.

Artichokes   There are very many ways of preparing *Artichokes*. They can be just cooked in salted water, and served with Hollandaise sauce (see page 121). They can be done in the Italian style—quartered and cooked in boiling water, then drained, browned in the oven in a little oil, arranged in a dish and covered with Parmesan cheese. They can be stuffed with shrimps. In this case boil the artichokes and hollow out; mix half a pound of shrimps with butter and cream, boil for a few minutes, and stuff the artichokes. Place the stuffed artichokes in a fireproof dish, sprinkle with chopped parsley and butter, and place in the oven. Serve very hot.

Artichokes à   To make *Artichokes à la Diable*, first boil the artichokes,
la Diable   then let them cool; then sprinkle with Cayenne pepper, dip in batter, fry, and serve hot.

Artichokes à la   For a cold artichoke dish, why not try *Artichokes à la*
President   *President*? Boil the artichokes and let them cool. Stuff them with ham mousse (see page 65), and cover with slices of hard-boiled eggs and slices of truffle. Brush over with aspic (see page 26), and serve cold.

Artichokes   *Artichokes Printaniers* make a very decorative dish.
Printaniers   Quarter small tender artichokes, and half-cook in water. Drain. Place in a fireproof dish, and add half a glass of white wine, veal or chicken stock, four or six small new carrots, green peas, six or eight new potatoes, four or six small tomatoes, and any French beans. Season with salt and pepper and chopped chives. Pour a quarter of a pint of cream over the top. Bake in the oven for thirty minutes, and serve in the same dish.

I am told that the aubergine comes from Turkey, but I know also that the Bulgarians grow it. They are the best gardeners I know of—they grow all kinds of vegetables in large quantities, and I am told that because they eat only vegetables they never die.

I love the look of *Aubergines*—or egg-plants, as they are sometimes called. I love their fine, shiny, purple colour. They also have a very delicate flavour, and make an ideal hors-d'œuvres or first course, especially when stuffed.

Stuffed Aubergines

Split the aubergine in half lengthwise, and put it in a baking tin. Cook in the oven for ten to fifteen minutes, until it is easy to remove the inside. Keep the skin firm. When the aubergine is cold, take out the inside, leaving the skin whole for stuffing.

For the stuffing, first try to remove the seeds from the inside of the aubergine. The seeds are not bad, but there are rather too many of them. When you have removed them, cut the inside of the aubergine into small pieces— dice if possible. Cut some spring onions finely, and fry in butter until golden-brown. Chop some mushrooms into small pieces, and add to the onions and fry with them for a few minutes. Cook some rice in a little salted water until tender. Mix the mushrooms, onions, and rice together with the inside of the aubergine. Add salt and pepper and enough cream to make it easy to stuff into the skin.

This dish can be served either hot or cold. If you want it hot, put the stuffed aubergine in the oven with a little additional cream. If you are serving it cold, sprinkle with a little Parmesan cheese.

There are many *Variations on the Theme of Stuffed Aubergines*. I had rather a good one in America. As usual, the aubergine is slit in half lengthwise. Then it is salted, allowed to drain for a few minutes, dried with a cloth, and fried thoroughly in hot oil for about ten minutes. Drain again, then scoop out the middle, being careful not to break the skin. Mash the flesh, adding a little garlic and

Variations on the Theme of Stuffed Aubergines

chopped dill and an equal amount of mushrooms—that is, the same amount as the aubergine. Season with salt and black pepper, mix together, and stuff into the aubergine skin. Sprinkle with breadcrumbs and butter or oil. Brown in the oven, and serve in a long dish with tomato sauce.

All sorts of different stuffings can be used for aubergines. Another alternative is a pound of onions, finely chopped and browned in about a quarter of a pound of butter, mixed with four skinned tomatoes and quite a lot of chopped dill. Again, sometimes I stuff aubergine with minced ham and eggs; or with minced veal and eggs; or with cheese and boiled fish. An excellent stuffing can be made by adding lobster-meat to chopped onions fried in butter, and mixing with some cream and quite a bit of chopped dill.

Here is another recipe, using half a pound of lobster-meat or scampi. Take three ounces of rice, wash very thoroughly, and boil in water for five minutes only. Chop a small onion finely, or, even better, grate it, and sauté in a little butter until golden-brown. Add to this the lobster or scampi, two ounces of chopped mushrooms, salt and red pepper, the rice, and some cream. Mix well. When you have stuffed the aubergines, sprinkle with cream and grated Parmesan cheese, place in the oven for fifteen to twenty minutes, and before serving sprinkle with chopped dill on top.

Fried Aubergines

Of course aubergine does not have to be stuffed. It is also very good fried and used as a garnish. Cut it in even round slices, add salt and pepper, then sprinkle with a little flour. Make a batter with a very little yeast, tip in the slices of aubergine, and fry in deep hot oil.

Another Aubergine Dish (Italian)

My last word on this interesting vegetable is a dish I had in Rome. For this you peel and quarter the aubergine lengthwise, salt, and allow to drain. Wipe with a cloth, roll in flour, and fry in oil. Place the pieces side by side in a fireproof dish. Boil tomatoes—allow one pound to three aubergines—skin, and mash slightly, then add salt, pepper, parsley, and a little crushed garlic, and cook in oil. Cover each slice of aubergine with the tomatoes, sprinkle with breadcrumbs and oil or butter, and simmer in a moderate oven for thirty-five minutes. Serve very hot in the same dish.

Mushrooms are a delicious vegetable—but, of course, they can be dangerous, poisonous killers. It is no doubt a pleasant pastime to walk in the fields and gather mushrooms, but don't do it unless you know what's what. The bad ones are the best-looking kind—very decorative. You cannot be too careful, and even the edible variety can be very harmful if they are not fresh.

I once read in an American magazine about a kind of mushroom that I would like to try. It is brown, and apparently was found by a tribe of Indians in Mexico who do not eat it but just chew it for their delight. Apparently these dry, brown mushrooms have a nasty bitter taste, but after being chewed for a while they have the same effect as opium. According to the story in the magazine, these mushrooms create a wonderful feeling: the person who chews them sees life in a series of marvellous pictures, through a rose-coloured hue. He remains fully conscious all the time. The effect is only for a few hours, but there are no unpleasant after-effects and it is not habit-forming.

I also read that a rich young American banker has given up his business and is devoting his whole time to the study of these miraculous mushrooms. I suppose he will make a miraculous business out of them, and then we shall hear more. Meanwhile—let us be satisfied with our own edible mushrooms, which I think are satisfying enough. I use them for flavouring whenever possible, and, of course, there are also many good mushroom dishes.

For stuffing you need big mushrooms. Wash and peel the heads, and hollow out as much as possible without breaking them. Fill them with a little onion, ham, or any minced meat or fish. Cover with breadcrumbs, sprinkle

Mushrooms

Stuffed Mushrooms

with butter, and bake in a very hot oven until golden-brown. Decorate with parsley.

Creamed
Mushrooms

For creaming use small white button mushrooms. Cook in butter seasoned with salt and black pepper. Make some Béchamel sauce (see page 117), add one-eighth of a pint of cream, and simmer gently. Sprinkle with a little lemon juice before serving.

Mushroom
Purée

For a purée take half a pound of mushrooms, add a little butter, and lemon-juice, season with salt and black pepper, and boil in water until the water has evaporated. Add a tablespoon of flour and four tablespoons of cream. Mix together, but do not allow to boil. Pass through a sieve, and place the mushroom purée in a shortcrust pastry shell, and sprinkle with chopped parsley before serving.

Fennel

Fennel is a vegetable eaten a great deal in the south of France. Personally I am not very keen on it, but in case you like it here is one way of doing it. You clean three or four of the vegetables, take off the hard outside leaves, then cut each fennel into four pieces. Boil for ten to fifteen minutes. Dry, and put together with chopped onions and four sliced tomatoes into a casserole. Pour on it a few tablespoons of stock, and put it in the oven for an hour. The French use garlic as well. I don't.

Nettles

Nettles, I am told, contain proteins, carbohydrates, and Vitamins A, B, and D. They also sting, like wasps, another pet aversion of mine. Between them wasps and nettles ruined my childhood joys in the garden. Even when I write the word I have painful itching memories, and nettles still stop me from gardening.

But please don't let me put you off from trying nettles as a vegetable. I have already described how a German friend taught me to pick them without getting stung—by putting your hands under instead of over the leaves—and compared with the picking everything else is easy. Use only young nettles, take a large bundle, and wash thoroughly, changing the water several times: it is wise to leave the leaves in cold water for a while. Dry, and chop the leaves finely, then put in a saucepan with a little cold water and salt. Cook slowly until tender. Put through a sieve. Melt an ounce of butter, add a tablespoon of flour, and mix with the purée. Add a few drops of lemon juice, a quarter of a pint of cream or milk, and a little black pepper. Then serve.

I have described how to make a soup from another weed, sorrel; and with its good savoury flavour, piquant and sour, it is also pleasant as a vegetable or a sauce. We used to have it as a vegetable with roast pork, duck, or goose, and as a sauce with boiled beef.

Here is one way of cooking *Sorrel* as a vegetable. Wash *Sorrel* two pounds of the weed very well, and boil in a very little salted water. Like other green vegetables if you want it to stay green you have to boil it uncovered. If, on the other hand, you want to retain more of the valuable vitamins at the expense of the green colour, you have to cover it very well. After boiling for ten minutes, drain and pass through a sieve. Mix a roux with a little butter and flour, and heat until it is golden-yellow; add to the sorrel, and braise in the oven. Before serving, mix two beaten egg-yolks with an eighth of a pint of cream, pour into the boiling sorrel, and stir vigorously.

My last vegetable is not a vegetable at all, but a nut: the *Chestnut*, which is used mostly as a sweet and also as a stuffing.

All good things have their disadvantages, and the worst *Chestnuts* thing about the chestnut is that it is a little bit difficult to skin. Difficult, but not impossible. If you want to keep them whole I think you will find you can do it this way. First make a slit round them with a very sharp knife, then place them in very warm fat; do not overheat it, as the chestnuts should not be browned. Now half-cook in water, drain, and peel. You will have to peel the chestnuts in a cloth, because they must be kept hot. The skins come off very easily in this way. Finally dry the chestnuts, and finish cooking in a good brown sauce.

If you want to use chestnuts for stuffing goose or duck, use the same method but allow the chestnuts to cook fully in the fat.

Chestnuts can also be used as a purée. In this case you have to add milk or cream to make the purée softer. Add salt, and black pepper or celery salt to taste.

CHAPTER NINE

SAUCES FOR EVER

WHEN I lived in York we often had guests for dinner. On one occasion we had a party of Quakers, the majority of whom were teetotallers. From previous experience I knew the drinks would have to be orange squash, lemon squash, and apple-juice—none of them very stimulating, so I thought I would try to make up for it in the cooking.

I cooked roast beef in red wine, made a cabbage salad with white wine, and served a light almond soufflé with a nice fresh cream rum sauce. To follow were pineapple slices, with a half orange in the centre of each slice and the whole thing swimming in Curaçao.

My efforts were rewarded, for the chief teetotaller said to his wife, "I just can't understand why an English cook cannot make nice sauces like these. We in England have fifty religions and three sauces."

For most Hungarians there was only one religion but well over fifty sauces, and on this branch of cooking I think we could go on talking or writing almost for ever. Sauces, I think, are highly personal things. They also seem an irresistible temptation to experiment. Whenever I make a sauce I do it in a different way each time, adding or taking away something so that it is never quite the same.

Of the classical sauces one of the most useful and best known is *Béchamel*. I use it often for many things—including soufflés; for it never happens that a soufflé made with a little Béchamel sauce collapses on you.

Sauce Béchamel (Simple)

There are several ways of making Béchamel sauce. A straightforward way is to melt about one ounce of butter

117

and add the same amount of flour, cook for just a few
minutes but keep it white, then add one pint of milk or
meat stock or fish stock, and stir with a whisk until it
boils. Season with salt and black or red pepper, and cook
on a slow flame for about quarter of an hour. From this
basic sauce many other sauces can be made by adding
various ingredients.

Sauce
Béchamel
(Elaborate)

For a more *Elaborate Béchamel Sauce*, melt butter in a
saucepan and add some clean carrots cut in small pieces,
the same amount of diced onions, some celeriac or celery,
and the same amount of finely sliced raw ham. Sauté the
vegetables in the butter for about ten to twelve minutes.
Be careful not to colour it—it must be kept a very light
colour. Afterwards take out the vegetables and ham, and
put them on a plate. Then melt more butter in the same
saucepan, add an equal amount of flour, and mix well.
Cook the butter and flour for just a few minutes, and add
the milk, stirring all the time. Put back the vegetables and
ham. Season with salt and white pepper and dill or tarragon
or any other herbs, and simmer for about an hour on a very
low flame. You can use this Béchamel sauce with any fish
or meat or cauliflower or anything else.

Asparagus
Sauce (Two
Recipes)

In the chapter on fish I suggested that if asparagus was
in season, boiled filleted plaice (see page 32) could be
very pleasant with an *Asparagus Sauce*. This is another
variation on the theme of Béchamel. Make a simple
Béchamel sauce with just butter, flour, and milk. When
cold, add two or three egg-yolks and some cream. Heat
but do not boil. Stir until smooth. Take off the stove and
add the asparagus, which should have been boiled and cut
into half-inch pieces. Season with salt and pepper. If you
like it piquant, add a little lemon juice.

II

Another Asparagus Sauce can be made with the rather
thin green asparagus that can be bought quite reasonably
in season. It has a good flavour, and when very thin I use
it for sauce or soup. I scrape the asparagus, and cut
it in small pieces, taking care to separate the tips. Then I

boil it all in a small saucepan with very little salted water in which I put a pinch of sugar. I take out the asparagus, put the tips aside, and pass the rest through a sieve. Next I make a roux from a little butter and flour, mix it well, add the asparagus water and sieved asparagus, and boil for another ten minutes. Then I add one or two egg-yolks and a little cream, put in the asparagus tips, and boil it up once more. If it is too thick I add a little chicken stock. This sauce can be served with meat, boiled chicken, fish, or indeed any dish.

The well-known *Mornay Sauce* is simply a Béchamel sauce with Parmesan or Gruyère cheese added. Before adding the cheese, take the sauce off the heat. It is better to use a wooden spoon for the mixing than a whisk. When the cheese and sauce are well mixed and seasoned, serve immediately. *Sauce Mornay*

Another classical sauce that I use a lot is *Remoulade of Mayonnaise*. Add some mustard, capers, gherkins, and finely chopped herbs to mayonnaise (see page 128). Dilute with the water in which you have cooked your herbs. Make it as thick or thin as you like. Season with pepper, salt, and a little sugar. *Remoulade of Mayonnaise*

Sauce Tartare can be made in all sorts of ways, but I still follow the way we had it at home. You pass two or three hard-boiled egg-yolks through a sieve into a china bowl, then you add two raw egg-yolks slowly with a few drops of lemon-juice—add them alternately, a little egg-yolk and then a little lemon-juice, again and again until the two egg-yolks are completely used. Season with salt and pepper, a little sugar, and French mustard. Work until creamy, then add half a pint of thick cream. Work it all the time, then add chopped parsley, chopped chives, chopped gherkins, and sometimes chopped capers. Chop the hard-boiled egg-whites very finely, and add them to the sauce. *Sauce Tartare*

To make a *Piquant Sauce*, chop some shallots and fry them in butter until they are a yellow colour, then add wine vinegar and boil until the liquid is reduced by half. *Sauce Piquant*

Add half a glass of white wine, and boil slowly for twelve to fifteen minutes. Before serving add some chopped gherkins, chopped parsley, and chopped chives.

Sauce Béarnaise   *Béarnaise* is another sauce you will find served in most good hotels and restaurants. Chop some shallots and put them in a saucepan with a glass of white wine, one and a half glasses of vinegar, some tarragon, some chopped chives, paprika, and salt. Bring to the boil, and simmer until the liquid is reduced by two-thirds. Stir until cool, then add two or three egg-yolks, stirring well. Put back on the stove, not over the flame but over a saucepan of boiling water; and add, piece by piece, about half a pound of butter. Beat the sauce with a whisk all the time. When the butter has all been added, beat for another few minutes, then the sauce is ready. It should be very light. Be careful never to let it boil, but just keep it warm. Chopped tarragon and chervil should be added. If you care for it, you can also add cayenne pepper—but very sparingly. Serve with any meat or egg dish.

White Chaudfroid   A very useful sauce for any kind of chicken or other bird, or any cold meat or fish, is the well-known *White Chaudfroid*. This is how I make it.

Prepare a white roux with butter and flour. Cook only for a very short time, and then add some very strong stock— chicken, veal or fish, depending on what you want to use the sauce for. Stir until it comes to the boil, and cook very slowly for one hour. Remove the scum from time to time. Add two or three egg-yolks and a fair amount of cream. Strain the sauce and allow it to cool, stirring from time to time to prevent a skin from forming on the surface.

Green Chaudfroid   You can make this sauce green by cooking a purée of spinach, watercress, chervil, and tarragon for a few minutes, and then adding this to the sauce—but only when the sauce is cold. If you want it pink, add tomato and red pepper.

Brown Chaudfroid   For a *Brown Chaudfroid* sauce, make a roux, heat it until it is a good golden-brown, and then add a strong brown stock with a little tomato purée. When it has boiled, remove the fat; then cook for an hour or so. After that add port or madeira wine and stir until it is cold.

One of the most famous—and justly so—of all sauces is the *Hollandaise*. Here, I think, an exception should be made over the matter of experimenting. It is such a perfect, clean sauce that I think it should not be played with but left alone. This is how I make it.

Sauce Hollandaise

Crush a few peppercorns, add a little vinegar and a drop of water, and boil until the liquid is reduced by half. Strain through a sieve and let it cool. Add four egg-yolks, and stir very vigorously. Whip up in a bain-marie until it becomes thick. Add half a pound of butter in small dots, a little salt, a little sugar, and some lemon-juice to finish off. Add herbs—parsley, chives, or any other—according to your taste, and heat. This sauce can be served with fish or any meat or asparagus, and can be served hot or cold. Instead of vinegar you may—I do—prefer lemon-juice.

For a *Tomato Sauce*, crush three or four pounds of ripe tomatoes and boil them for five or six minutes. Pass through a sieve, then put back on the fire and add two ounces of butter, a pinch of salt, a little sugar, and a little milk or cream.

Tomato Sauce (Two Recipes)

Alternatively you can make a good *Tomato Sauce* from tinned tomato purée. Grate some small onions, and sauté them in a little butter. Add just a soupçon of garlic, sprinkle a spoonful of flour on the onions, and with this make a roux. Keep it light, add the tomato purée, and pour milk on it, then add salt and sugar, as much as you like—I like mine definitely sweet. Instead of milk you can use cream or a good chicken stock.

II

Two of my favourite hot sauces are dill sauce and horse-radish sauce.

Dill is my favourite herb. I think it has a delicious flavour. It goes very well with boiled beef or any fowl. Make a roux with a very little lard and flour. Heat for three to five minutes, taking care not to let it colour. Add

Dill Sauce

meat or chicken stock, stir over the flame, and boil for two or three minutes. Add a little vinegar, sugar, and salt. Then add quite a lot of chopped dill and one or two egg-yolks beaten in a little cream. Do not let it boil any more, but serve hot. If you do not like sour sauce, just leave out the vinegar—I often do.

Horse-radish Sauce (Two Recipes)   Begin horse-radish sauce in the same way. Make a roux with very little fat—if possible, chicken fat or lard—and a little flour. Heat and stir, but do not let it get brown. Add salt and a little sugar, then some water, and boil for five minutes. Now take a good-sized horse-radish, wash and scrub it, grate it and sprinkle a little salt on it immediately. Salt keeps it white. Put it in the boiling sauce, but do not let it boil any more. Horse-radish gets bitter if it is boiled. Serve with boiled fowl or any beef. This sauce has to be served hot.

II   For *Another Horse-radish Sauce*, grate a piece of horse-radish, put it in a bowl, and salt immediately; then add a tablespoon of English mustard and two tablespoons of wine vinegar, a tablespoon of sugar, half a pint of cream, and two or three tablespoons of white breadcrumbs (soaked previously in milk). Mix well, and serve cold.

For boiled beef or any cold meat, apple purée mixed with horse-radish is a very excellent cold sauce. For bigger occasions I make an ice bombe or parfait by simply adding whipped cream to the horse-radish sauce and freezing it.

Redcurrant Sauce   Another sauce that I like with boiled beef is made from preserved *Redcurrants*. Boil them up in the same sweet juice in which they have been preserved. Mix a little cream with one or two egg-yolks, and pour the hot sauce on this. Serve hot or cold. The same thing can be done with preserved gooseberries.

Cumberland Sauce   *Cumberland Sauce* is a favourite of mine. For this, chop some shallots and boil them in water. Add some orange or lemon peel, cut very finely, boil a few minutes more, and pour through a sieve. Mix the liquid with melted red-currant jelly—if possible home-made—and some red wine or port. Add a little orange or lemon juice and, if you like, a little English mustard.

I am also fond of *Cranberry Sauce*, which is very good for any poultry, ham, or game. You can buy the fruit nearly the whole year through, but usually I buy a large quantity in October, when it is cheapest. Boil the lovely red berries in sugar and water, and simmer for ten or fifteen minutes. The berries burst very quickly; the sauce should be thick but still liquid. It should be a little sweet but piquant.

Cranberry Sauce

You will not have heard of *Sauce Pierre*, because I have given it this name. It is not my invention—I have christened it after its creator, a well-known bachelor gourmet who taught me how to make it at his home in the south of France. It is quite easy to make, and a very useful sauce that can be used for many dishes: one of those things, in fact, that you should always have in your refrigerator.

Sauce Pierre

You need equal portions of carrots, onions, and ham, a few sprigs of parsley, and any herbs you like—thyme, tarragon, or dill. Cut these ingredients in pieces, and brown them in a little fat or butter—again the same weight as the ham. Add two or three tablespoons of flour, mix well, and continue to heat until the flour is golden-brown. Add a glass of white wine and two or three tablespoons of thick tomato purée, two or three chopped mushrooms, and, if you have it, some chicken or veal stock —if you haven't any, water will do. Simmer very gently for an hour and a half or so, skimming the sauce from time to time. Then strain into another saucepan, put back on the heat, bring to the boil, and skim once more; the sauce should be absolutely free from fat. Now let it reduce to about one-third, and lastly add two or three tablespoons of Madeira wine—the amount is according to your taste. After putting it in the refrigerator, take off the remaining fat if there is any left.

Sauce Isabella comes from Italy, where I have enjoyed it with tournedos. You need white wine—preferably

Sauce Isabella

a slightly sour wine—and I use two wineglasses of it with one chopped shallot. Put the wine and the shallot into a saucepan, together with some chopped tarragon, and add a little salt and paprika. Let it come to the boil, then simmer slightly until the liquid has reduced. Remove from the heat and allow to cool; then add three egg-yolks, and stir well. Next put this saucepan in a larger saucepan containing boiling water, and very gradually add about half a pound of butter, piece by piece, beating with an egg whisk all the time. It should be a very light sauce. I serve chopped chives with it. If your wine is not sour enough, a little lemon juice is very refreshing. It is easy to make—but there is one important thing: don't let it boil. If you don't like chopped shallots in the sauce, strain it before serving.

Parmesan Sauce   *Parmesan Sauce* is excellent for lobster. Take a quarter of a pound of butter, two tablespoons of flour, a little salt and paprika; stir for two minutes over the heat, then pour half a pint of milk on it and let it boil for another minute. Take it off the heat, and stir into it three tablespoons of grated Parmesan cheese and two egg-yolks. Put it back on the heat, but don't let it boil—just stir vigorously until it is smooth, and then pour it on the lobster.

Shrimp Sauce   *Shrimp Sauce* is excellent with a cheese soufflé (see page 137), among other things. Grate a small onion and fry it in butter, and immediately add salt. The onion should not get crisp but must be soft. Put in a little paprika, then the shrimps. Stir for a few minutes, and add a little fish stock or water. Boil, then add thick cream. Chopped dill improves this sauce.

Half-glaze Sauce   For a *Half-glaze Sauce*, make a roux of lard or chicken fat and flour, and cook very slowly, stirring from time to time, until it is a nice brown colour; then add some brown stock and tomato purée, and stir until it starts to boil. Turn down the flame and let it boil very slowly for two to three hours. Skim from time to time to get rid of the fat and scum. Finally strain and put it in a jar. When cool, put in the refrigerator, and just use it when you need it.

CHAPTER TEN

THE SALAD AND THE DRESSING

SOME days I have to make up to half a dozen different menus for lunches or dinners. This is not a great problem for, like everything else, it is just a matter of developing a technique. So as a rule it does not worry me much, and often I can settle it all on the spur of the moment. But if I have to find a lot of different salads—for example, for a buffet for five or six hundred people—then I know I am in for a spell of hard searching and thinking.

Salads have always been of great importance in any meal, today more than ever, in this age of slimming and vitamins. They need to look decorative and refreshing and interesting and to match or harmonise with the other food on the menu. In a buffet a salad has to be nearly as colourful and eye-pleasing as the flower or fruit baskets. It should also taste good!

Which brings me, before the salads, to the salad dressing.

Take three parts of oil to one part of vinegar, add a little lemon or lime juice, season with salt and pepper or paprika, and you have—yes, of course: *French Salad Dressing*, the most famous, the basic dressing that is used throughout the world.

French Salad Dressing

At least, you have one version of it. (Actually it is an American version.) It would take a chapter, if not a whole book, to give all the other versions of this classic recipe. The same applies to the other world-famous dressing, the mayonnaise; and, to a slightly lesser extent, to Hollandaise sauce (see page 121). Wherever I go—whether to a private house, a restaurant, or a hotel—small or grand, cheap or expensive—the salad dressings are never the same. Every chef or maître d'hotel, every cook, man or woman, takes something out or puts something in and in one way or another makes it different.

There are, of course, hundreds of possible variations on the basic recipes—hundreds of ways of improving or ruining the dressing. I find some variations are very good, some not too bad, some very bad, some uneatable. But this is only my opinion. I find also that the people who make and consume these different dressings all swear that theirs is the best and, as a matter of fact, the only one worth eating.

Thousands of years ago a clever man made the shrewd observation that there is no arguing about tastes. This applies particularly to salad dressings, and I would not dream of arguing about them. As in most matters of food, people generally tend to like what they are used to, especially what they were brought up on. Nobody can cook as well as Mother or, as people used to say, "as we have it at home". I know this from my own experience. If I am ever asked to cook a dish or bake a cake—"you know, as Mother used to do once, it was wonderful"—I quickly interrupt that I will do my best, but I cannot hope to compete with Mother. I could never achieve the same flavour in my cooking as I had it at home. I try to copy it from memory, but it is never the same as my mother used to do it. Hers was much better!

I have just remembered a little story from my childhood. We had a very young kitchen maid, whose job was to run about for the cook. The cook was a nice, huge woman, and an excellent cook; but only now have I realized that she must have been a drunkard, because sometimes grave disasters happened in the kitchen that upset my very house-proud mother. I particularly remember one lunch-time, when my mother smelt a very unpleasant kitchen smell in the house—a burning smell—so she went out in the kitchen and immediately noticed what had happened. A panful of creamed vegetable marrow had burnt, and that was the cause of the unpleasant smell.

My mother, a little angrily, ordered the cook to throw the whole dish in the dustbin and make something new quickly. The little kitchen-maid was terrified of the cook but liked my mother. She went to her and asked if she could please have the whole dish of vegetable marrow herself. "It has such a lovely smell," she said, "exactly the same as my mother used to do it at home, and I would just love to eat it all." She came from the mountains, in a part of Hungary where the very poor Roumanians lived, and I suppose her mother cooked on an open fire and everything was either burnt or uncooked—but for her the burnt vegetable marrow had a lovely flavour, because it was as Mother made it.

Much the same thing happened when some school-children from York went to Paris. Several of them were sons of my friends. When they came back I asked them how they liked Paris. "Oh," they said, "Paris is a very beautiful city—but the food! We could not wait to come home!"

Recently my son brought a friend home—again a boy from York. When they left, the boy told my son, "You know, whenever I am in your people's home I leave the house hungry. The dishes are so unusual. Even the butter is unsalted."

All this may not seem to have much to do with salads and salad dressings, but I just wanted to explain why I shall not try to tell you how a salad dressing ought to be made. You go ahead and be daring—and for all you know you may hit on something brilliant, and then a lot of people will be thankful and you will go down in culinary history as immortal.

In case you are less ambitious, here is something you can try with French salad dressing. It is called *Roquefort Dressing*, for quite obvious reasons. Take half a cupful of

Roquefort Dressing

ordinary French dressing, and beat into it one tablespoon of tarragon, wine-vinegar, two tablespoons of tomato ketchup, four tablespoons of olive oil, about two or three ounces of crumbled Roquefort cheese, one teaspoon of grated onion or half a teaspoon of minced chives.

Mayonnaise

Mayonnaise is often regarded with unnecessary awe, and quite a lot of people are afraid to make it. In fact it is simply and quickly made. You take two or three egg-yolks, and add a pinch of salt, white or black pepper, and lemon-juice. Start to whip the egg-yolks vigorously with a whisk, adding, drop by drop, a good fresh olive oil. When the sauce starts to thicken, the oil may be added more quickly. Beat continuously, from time to time adding a few drops of lemon-juice. If, when the mayonnaise is finished, you find it too thick, add two or three tablespoons of hot water and a little sugar.

Alternatively, use hard-boiled instead of raw egg-yolks. Again add salt, pepper, and lemon-juice, whisk in a bowl, and add lukewarm oil drop by drop. Just before finishing add a very little boiling water.

Long Island Salad Dressing

If you like mayonnaise you may care to try *Long Island Salad Dressing*. Take one cupful of mayonnaise, and add two tablespoons of chilli sauce, two tablespoons of minced stuffed olives, one tablespoon of chopped green pepper, one tablespoon of minced onions or chives, and a quarter to half a cupful of heavy cream, whipped or plain.

One important point: whatever dressing you make, if oil has to be used at all it should be the best olive oil. Personally I use it very sparingly as I do not like it much, although I know that in this respect I am in the minority. That is why I like Hollandaise and Cumberland and cranberry sauces. I never make chicory, lettuce, or tomato salad with oil, but use only lemon-juice and a little sugar. I find this much lighter and more pleasant than any heavy oil dressing—but again, each to his taste.

So much for the dressing in general: now for some particular salads.

I think the most popular is *Potato Salad*. You can have
it with mayonnaise and a lot of chives mixed in, or you can
make it with only vinegar and a little sugar. Personally,
again, I never use anything but lemon juice with sugar,
chives, and chopped parsley.

Celeriac Salad has a most delicate and delightful flavour.
You peel the celeriac very carefully, cut it in very even
slices, and boil it in lemon-flavoured water with a little
salt. Make a dressing from lemon juice with a little sugar,
and mix it well. Leave it in the refrigerator for two hours,
and decorate it with cut tomato and shredded lettuce.

Aubergine Salad is justly popular. Boil the aubergine
and slice it thinly, as you would slice a cucumber; and
then mix the slices with some very thinly sliced (and
peeled) cucumber, also skinned and sliced tomatoes and
finely chopped spring onions or chives. Sprinkle with a
very little olive oil if you like it, and make a dressing from
lemon-juice and sugar, diluted with water according to
your taste. Chill in the refrigerator before serving.

For *Asparagus and Mushroom Salad*, first skin the
asparagus and boil until tender; then cut it into small
pieces, leaving the tops separate. The mushrooms should
be very small button mushrooms, and you have to boil
them in lemon-juice to keep them snow-white. Add the
asparagus and mushrooms to mayonnaise or Hollandaise
or some other sauce, and mix together. Put the asparagus
heads on top, and decorate with any kind of green.

Japanese Salad is both tasty and decorative. Take some
lettuces and put the hearts on one side, wash the leaves well
and place them in a wooden bowl. Add chicory cut in small
pieces, very finely sliced cucumber (peeled or unpeeled),
a few very tiny peeled tomatoes—these should be no
bigger than small radishes—and every kind of fruit you
can lay your hands on: peaches, apricots, apples, pears,
pineapple, and any other fruit. Next put in all the lettuce
hearts. (If they are big, cut them into four pieces; if they
are small, leave them whole.) Now mix some cream

Potato Salad

Celeriac Salad

Aubergine Salad

Asparagus and Mushroom Salad

Japanese Salad

cheese with a little cream and salt, and make as many little balls as you have guests. Add a few pieces of pineapple. Make a dressing from the pineapple-juice and lemon-juice, and sugar to taste, and pour it in the wooden bowl. Hard-boil two or three eggs, and pass the yolks through a sieve, covering the whole dish. You will find that this salad tastes as good as it looks, and that is very good indeed.

Russian Salad

We often come across *Russian Salad* on a menu, but it is very rarely a real Russian salad. Usually it is made from all kinds of vegetable—potatoes, carrots, celery, celeriac, peas and green beans. For a genuine Russian salad you must also add beef, pork, salami, anchovy, and, if you can, caviare, all mixed together and decorated with tomatoes, radishes, and hard-boiled eggs.

Apple and Celery Salad

Apple and Celery Salad is interesting. Take a very small amount of citric acid powder—about half a coffee-spoonful —and put this into the salad bowl or dish. Add a tin of condensed milk, then add a little more citric acid powder and sugar according to your taste. The citric acid makes the milk very thick. I always add a good spoonful of orange marmalade, too. Now take equal amounts of celery and apples, cut them in very even round slices, and put them into the bowl or dish and mix together. Add a handful of cashew nuts and as much grated horse-radish as you like. Place chopped lettuce and tomato slices round the dish for decoration.

Orange Salad

An *Orange Salad* is very quickly made and goes well with most roast birds.

First peel some oranges, and be sure to take off the pith. You must have a pointed knife—a very sharp one, too. Sharp knives and other kitchen tools need to be of the best quality; efficiency is not acquired by having all the available gadgets in the kitchen, but by making sure that the equipment you do buy is of first-class quality and by keeping it in good condition. But back to the orange salad. When peeling the oranges, keep the peel from one, shred it very finely, and boil it in water until tender, then put it in a syrup and boil it for another ten minutes. Cut the oranges in either round slices or sections, making sure that no skin or pith remains on them and, of course, removing all the pips. Put the slices or sections of the oranges in a glass dish. Boil two ounces of sugar in a quarter of a pint of water and add this to the syrup in which the orange peel was boiled; adding, when the syrup is cold, a glass of sherry and as much rum or arrack as you like. Pour this liquid over the orange slices or sections. Decorate the dish with prunes which have first been stoned and stuffed with peeled almonds or cashew nuts. Cut the orange peel, already boiled in sugar, into small pieces and decorate the top of the dish. Shredded lettuce also can be added as decoration.

During the war, when delicacies were rare, I used to make a *Prune Salad* from time to time which I think is still worth the trouble now that the shortages have disappeared. Soak the prunes for twenty-four hours, then remove the stones and replace them with almonds or cashew nuts. Put the prunes in a glass dish, and pour over them a good syrup with quite a generous addition of rum or arrack. Put the dish in the refrigerator for a few hours, and decorate with shredded lettuce. *Prune Salad*

An interesting salad can be made with peaches and pears in equal quantities. Simmer them in syrup for a few minutes, cover with a very piquant mayonnaise, and decorate with lettuce leaves. *Peach and Pear Salad*

One of the best salads I ever tasted was in a private house in Vienna, actually the American Ambassador's house. The whole dinner was exquisite, but the first course was the most memorable of all. It looked like a beautiful river fish—I thought at once of the famous Hungarian schullo without knowing what it was. It was covered with tartare sauce and decorated very neatly with elegant, quiet taste. When I cut into the fish I found out that it was a fish salad. *A Fish Salad*

The snow-white meat of the fish had been taken off the

carcass, mixed with tartare sauce, cooked green peas, cooked and diced beetroot, finely chopped celery, cooked and shredded celeriac, gherkins, very finely cut apples, and very finely shredded white and red cabbage; and then put back on the carcass of the fish and covered with more thick tartare sauce.

CHAPTER ELEVEN

EGGS AND CHEESE

ONCE back in Hungary a poor young artist told me, happily, that he had found a way to keep his independence. He would not have to prostitute his art for his stomach after all, he said, for he had found out eggs went much farther if you put in one or two onions. Onions were extremely cheap in Hungary. He told me that he had two eggs with two or three onions for his midday dinner, and felt fine and very well fed.

There is everything to be said for eggs. They are nourishing and light—and excellent as invalid food—and the most wonderful stand-by for emergencies. You will never be embarrassed when invaded by unexpected guests if you have plenty of eggs in your larder. They are quick and easy to cook, and can be used in an almost infinite variety of ways. Cold or hot, savoury or sweet—literally hundreds of different dishes can be made. You only have to change the seasoning or the flavours and you have a different dish. One could live on eggs for weeks and weeks without ever getting tired of them. If one set one's mind to it, it should be possible to make different egg dishes three times a day for a whole year without repeating any of them.

The subject is so large, indeed, that whole books have been written consisting of nothing but egg dishes. Every general cookery book has quite a substantial chapter on cooking with eggs. It hardly seems necessary for me to try to add anything—and besides, even without all these recipes, everybody can cook eggs in quite a number of excellent ways. What is there, for example, to beat a fresh egg just boiled in its shell for three minutes? Of course for this the egg has to be really fresh—for my taste, not older than twenty-four hours. Again, nothing could be easier or nicer than a plain simple egg with two tablespoons of water added, and in the frying-pan just enough butter to ensure that the pan will not be dry—into the pan with the egg, stir it only a very few times, and serve on a well-heated plate.

Yes, whatever you do, heat the plate; and I am not thinking only of egg dishes now. This is one of my hobby-horses. Hot dishes should be served hot on heated plates, and cold dishes and cold drinks should be served ice-cold—or not served at all. When I was last in the south of Italy I was very annoyed because the food—which was not very good, anyway—was made even less palatable by being served on luke-warm plates. When I complained to the waiter he smiled and said, "But what for hot food? The weather is warm."

Omelettes   The champion of the egg dishes is, of course, the omelette. It is said that it is an art to make a good *Omelette*, even if it is a very simple one. I would say that perhaps it requires a little skill, but anybody should be able to learn it. You only have to be a little careful and think what you are doing and not of what you have to do later in the evening or the next day.

The most important thing is the pan. It should be a heavy iron one, as this will retain enough heat to cook the omelette quickly. I remember that in my mother's house our very good cook had an iron frying pan which was never washed, and if anybody had dared to use it for anything else but an omelette there would have been terrible trouble. She never made an omelette with more than three eggs at the most, but she preferred making separate omelettes with two eggs for every person, and used to send them to the table one by one at very quick intervals. They were lovely and light and had unforgettable flavours.

There are different schools of thought about omelette-making. One argument is about the mixing. Some people mix with a fork, and only so that the yolk breaks, and then just stir for a minute. Others like a whisk. Our cook used a fork, and so do I.

Another omelette argument is whether the flavouring should be added to the eggs when mixed or when the omelette is ready for folding. I support both sides. For the sake of variety, sometimes do it one way, adding the flavouring to the eggs, and sometimes the other way, when the omelette is ready for folding.

Our cook made omelettes with literally hundreds of flavours—and you can do the same. Cheese, ham, crisply fried bacon, mushroom, all kinds of vegetable, any kind of fish or meat—there is no limit to the possibilities.

Multiple Omelette

Sometimes for a first course, when there were about twelve of us at table, our cook used to make a sort of *Multiple Omelette*, which we do ourselves now when we have a lot of guests. First you make a plain omelette with four eggs—but don't fold it, just put it flat on a round dish standing on a saucepan containing boiling water. Spread on top shrimps mixed with a little cream. For the next omelette add, say, already boiled green peas. Then another plain omelette, then one with chopped ham mixed with a little cream; another plain one, then yet another, this time with chopped mushrooms fried with onions; yet one more plain omelette, and, on top, an omelette with grated Parmesan. Serve with burnt hot butter—quickly!

Savoury Pancakes

Another good egg dish is the *Savoury Pancake*. Make an ordinary pancake batter (see page 188), but leave out all the sugar and put in a little more salt. Cook the pancake in the usual way, and fill it with chopped ham mixed with a little cream and one egg-yolk to bind. After filling, roll up the pancakes and put them in a fireproof dish nicely, one next to the other. Make a little sauce with butter and flour, and add to it fresh cream, a little salt, and as much grated cheese as you like. Be careful not to stir too much after adding the cheese, or it will get rubbery. Pour the sauce on the pancakes, and put the dish in a hot oven or under the grill for a few minutes.

You can also make savoury pancakes with lobster. Mix and cook the pancakes in the same way, and then fill them with a mixture of lobster-meat, a little cream, beaten egg-yolk, salt, and black pepper. Finally sprinkle with grated cheese.

For cheese pancakes the filling is a very thick Béchamel sauce with plenty of Parmesan cheese, cream, and a whole egg. Sprinkle the top of the pancake with grated cheese and chopped dill.

Savoury Pancake (Hungarian)   In Hungary we had another *Savoury Pancake*. For this we made the batter a little more liquid, and mixed into it a whole head of cabbage that had been chopped very finely and browned in lard and black pepper. The cabbage needs to be very well browned. Put a very little lard in the pancake pan—just enough to make it greasy—and try to make the pancakes as thin as possible. Cook on both sides and roll up. When all the pancakes are ready, put them in a hot oven before serving. Serve hot and crisp.

Baked Eggs   *Baked Eggs* make an excellent first course or main dish. You have to buy nice decorative small individual or large fireproof dishes. Pour a little cream in the bottom of each. When the cream is hot, drop in an egg or as many eggs as you wish. Then add asparagus—either tinned or, if fresh, already boiled—sliced mushroom that has been sautéd with a little onion, or just cream, butter, ham or any other meat. Put back in the oven for a few minutes, and serve.

Poached Eggs (Two Recipes)   *Poached Egg* is, I think, greatly improved by the addition of cheese. Boil some water in a saucepan, with a very little vinegar. Break a fresh egg on a plate, put a little salt on the yolk, and slide it quickly into the boiling water. When the water starts boiling again, move the saucepan to the side and let the egg poach without boiling for about two minutes. The time, of course, depends on how you like your poached egg, but the yolk should always be left soft. Do not cook too many eggs at one time. After poaching, drain and arrange the eggs on a dish—a buttered dish, if you like. Make a light, well-seasoned Béchamel sauce (see page 117), pour it on the eggs, and sprinkle with any kind of grated cheese. Put the dish under the grill and keep it there until nice and brown.

Another good way of doing *Poached Eggs* is with fried *II* ham and cheese sauce. Put slices of ham in hot butter, and fry on each side for one or two minutes. Peel and seed and chop tomatoes, cut green peppers in cubes and very carefully clean out the pips and veins, and sauté the tomatoes and peppers together. Poach as many eggs as there are persons to be served. Put the poached eggs on the hot slices of ham, and cover the eggs with the sautéd tomatoes and peppers. Make a white sauce with butter and flour and cream, add grated cheese—preferably Gruyère—pour it on each egg to cover, and brown under the grill.

Now here is how I make a *Cheese Soufflé*. *Cheese*

Melt two ounces of butter in a pan, and mix in the same *Soufflé* amount of flour. Stir for just a minute, then add half a pint of milk, salt, and a little paprika. Bring to the boil and simmer, stirring all the time with a whisk, until it starts to thicken, then take it off the fire. Stir into it another two ounces of butter and four to five egg-yolks, and mix well. Beat the egg-whites very stiff, fold them into the mixture together with four to five ounces of grated Gruyère or Parmesan cheese, and mix very carefully. Butter a fireproof dish, pour in the mixture, and bake in a moderate oven for twenty to twenty-five minutes. Serve immediately. The guest has to wait, not the soufflé.

Serve with either a mushroom sauce—this is simply a Béchamel sauce (see page 117) with plenty of mushrooms added—or shrimp sauce (see page 124).

Fondue is very fashionable now, especially at cocktail *Fondue* parties, so I shall give a little hint on how to make it. Very long ago I ate it in France. It is very easy to make, only the timing has to be watched—but this applies to every dish that includes eggs. For six people you need three eggs. Beat them very well together, add four ounces of cheese— grated Parmesan is the best—and two ounces of butter, salt, and red pepper. The butter should be added in small pieces and mixed all the time. Put on a high flame, and stir vigorously—be quick, or it will go rubbery—until it looks like a thick cream. Pour in a warm but not too hot dish, and serve immediately.

CHAPTER TWELVE

RICE AND OTHER CEREALS

NOWHERE on earth is rice pudding cooked better than in England. Wherever I have had it, in restaurants or hotels or private homes, it has always been lovely and creamy and quite unbeatable. Which makes it all the stranger that English people do not eat more savoury rice dishes as well. It is an excellent food, and very nourishing—millions of people in China and India live on it. It is used for a lot of savouries on the Continent, and deserves to be in England too.

Savoury Rice

It is very important first that it should be thoroughly washed and secondly that it should be cooked in the right way. Wash the rice in water at least ten times. Then let it dry. Sauté some very finely chopped or grated onions, with a very small piece of garlic pressed through the garlic presser; add the rice, stir continuously for five to eight minutes, then add salt and chicken or beef stock and cook for fifteen to twenty minutes. If you have no stock you can use water instead. In either case the amount of liquid should be double the amount of the rice—one cup of rice to two of liquid is a good rule. Be very careful with the cooking—it is easy to spoil by cooking a few minutes too little or too much. Before serving add chopped parsley generously.

Turkish Pilau

One of the most popular rice dishes is the *Turkish Pilau* or pilaff. There are many versions of this, according to the materials you use. First chop a large onion very finely, and brown it lightly in lard. When it is golden-brown add the

rice, and brown again for two or three minutes. Then add
the necessary stock and seasoning, some tomato purée, an
ounce of sultanas, an ounce of nuts, an apple cut in slices,
two or three sliced mushrooms, and any kind of meat—
chicken, giblets, veal, lamb, etc.—that has first been cut
into pieces and sautéd with onions until half cooked. The
volume of stock should be twice the volume of rice. Boil
until the rice is nearly cooked, and then add a little saffron.
Be very careful with this as it has a very strong flavour—
it is good in moderation but can be overpowering. I always
dilute saffron in warm water, then add a little while I am
stirring the pilaff, taste it, and if necessary add more. If
pimento is available, put in some of this too. Serve with
grated Parmesan cheese and tomato sauce.

Instead of meat you can make a pilaff with lobster or
scampi or any other fish.

Italian   Now here is my recipe for the world-famous *Italian*
Risotto   *Risotto*.

Wash the rice thoroughly, let it dry, then fry in butter
and boil in chicken stock for about twenty minutes. Cut
about half a pound of veal in small pieces and sauté in
butter with salt and black pepper until half done. Cut a few
mushrooms in slices, and sauté in butter. Chop some
cooked ham in small slices. Boil half a pound of spaghetti—
don't cook it too much—and drain. Put all these things
aside. Make a dough from two and a half ounces of butter,
four ounces of flour, one egg-yolk, salt, and a tablespoon
of wine. Roll out the dough. Take a round baking tin, butter
it well, and line it with the dough. Mix together a
pint of cream, about four ounces of butter, and a few
chopped capers. Now into the round baking tin, lined with
dough, put a layer of rice, a layer of ham on it, then a few
sliced mushrooms, a layer of spaghetti, and a layer of
diced veal, and pour on this some of the mixture of cream,
butter, and capers. Repeat the whole process, layer on
layer, and continue repeating it till the dish is full. Put in
the oven and bake till nice and brown, then turn out on a

hot round dish. Before serving, sprinkle with grated
Parmesan. If you like it, serve with a tomato sauce (see
page 121).

The Indians cook very good rice. An Indian friend of   *Indian Rice*
mine taught me her way of doing it. First wash the rice
in a lot of water—and to make sure it is well washed, put
half a tablespoon of flour in the rice when it is still dry, mix
it well, and then start the washing. Wash it four or five
times, using fresh water each time. Then put the rice into
a large saucepan of boiling salted water, and cook on a
very hot fire for eighteen minutes. Drain, cool, and dry
and reheat slowly with a little salted butter and black
pepper.

Many rice dishes can be used as a garnish or a vegetable.   *Rice Garnish*
Here is an example of a rice that will go well with many
different dishes. Finely chop one small onion, and soften it
in a little lard. Add paprika and salt. Add a well-washed
cup of rice and two cups of water or meat stock. Boil.
Sauté in butter a cup of young peas, and mix these with the
rice. Serve with a shrimp sauce (see page 124) poured over
the rice.

Hungarian peasants discovered long ago—by instinct,
no doubt—that even starches of the same group have more
nutritional value if they are eaten together. Hence the
various Hungarian dishes, both sweet and savoury, in
which potato is mixed with flour. Now my son George
tells me that some Asians have made the same discovery.
When he was in Hong Kong he was served the ordinary
savoury rice mixed with toasted squares of bread. Food-
values apart, this certainly makes the dish more interesting.

When I think of cereals I very soon begin to think of
Italy and its fantastic varieties of pasta. Then I think of
Rome, and the famous restaurant of Alfonso's. An Italian
friend introduced me to Alfonso, telling him a few words
about what I do in England; whereupon Alfonso invited us
to lunch and asked to be allowed to arrange the menu for
us. Naturally we were delighted.

While we were waiting, in order that we should not be
bored our host brought to our table a whole library of
Visitors' Books. I have never seen such a collection. They
were huge books, bound in leather, containing the signa-
tures of important and less important people from everywhere in the world. They had all written high praise of the
cooking at the restaurant, and many of them had stuck in
banknotes. In these books you could find currency from all
over the world. It seems that Signor Alfonso has never
been in need of money, for he has kept a considerable
amount stuck in his books as souvenirs.

When we had finished with the books he brought in the
lunch. The most memorable dish was the pasta—freshly
cooked noodles in a large bowl, into which Alfonso stirred
big lumps of fresh butter and a lot of Parmesan cheese.
Using his two famous golden spoons, he stirred and stirred,
adding more Parmesan, more butter, raising it higher and
higher—and this went on for at least fifteen minutes. It
looked beautiful. Then he dished it out—for my two
friends on their plates, but as I was the guest I got the
dish. I have never tasted such lovely noodles in my life.

Noodles

Noodles can be bought—but you cannot beat real home-
made egg noodles; and they are so easy to make. Take
two pounds of white flour, three to four eggs (or, say, three
eggs and one extra yolk), a little olive oil, salt, and as
much water as necessary—but be sure to make the dough
pretty stiff. Knead it together, leave to rest for an hour,
then roll out very thinly. Let it dry out a little, and cut.

Ravioli

Ravioli can be made with the same dough. The filling
can be any meat; for example, pieces of chicken, veal, pork,
and calf's brain all minced and then mixed with egg-yolk
to bind and a little bread or crumbs if you like. Alternatively ravioli can be filled with spinach. Another of our
fillings at home was calf's lights, which were first boiled
in salted water, then minced and mixed with a little cream
and an egg and well seasoned with black pepper and salt.
We used this ravioli as a garnish for chicken soup. When

serving ravioli by itself, after boiling, drain well, mix with butter, or oil or fat, and sprinkle with plenty of grated cheese.

You do not need to go to Sicily to eat macaroni *Stufati à la Siciliana*. Make it yourself. You need a large round dish about three inches deep, and the first thing you do is butter the bottom and sides generously. Then line the whole dish (bottom and sides) with aubergine cut in very thin slices. Now boil some medium-sized macaroni in salted water for ten minutes. Drain, put in a saucepan, and mix with butter. Then put one layer of macaroni in the dish with the aubergine, and sprinkle generously with Parmesan cheese. Meanwhile you should have skinned some tomatoes and sautéd them with salt in oil or butter. Now pepper some of these and put them on the dish. Add another layer of macaroni, more Parmesan cheese, and again the tomato; and repeat until the dish is full. Put cheese and butter on the top. Place in the oven for a whole hour. Remove from the dish, and serve very hot. It should look like a big cake. Its appearance is improved with some of the thin aubergine slices on the top. Serve with a thick tomato sauce and Parmesan cheese.

Stufati à la Siciliana

Here is *Another Macaroni Dish* that I enjoyed in Italy. Cook, but not completely, half a pound of fine macaroni in salted water. Drain while still slightly firm. Put one glass of Madeira wine in a saucepan with half a pint of tomato sauce, add two ounces of cooked ham, two ounces of cooked minced veal, and four cooked chopped mushrooms; and mix them all together. Add salt and pepper. Add to the macaroni. Cook for another fifteen minutes, then work a quarter of a pound of butter with a little flour and add to the mixture. Bring to the boil, take off the flame, and add three or four ounces of grated cheese. Serve as garnish or main dish.

Another Macaroni Dish

Most kinds of pasta are eaten as separate dishes, but I always think of nockerli—or *Gnocchi*, as the Italians and most other people call them—in connection with stews.

Gnocchi

C.F.L.—L

When we had a goulash at home in the old days it was never served without nockerli, and I regard them as belonging to the dumpling family.

Mix together half a pound of flour, a small piece of lard or butter—about the size of a walnut—two or three eggs, and a pinch of salt. Add a little water, taking care not to make the dough very soft; but it must not be too hard, either. Work with a wooden spoon till smooth—don't overwork it—and leave it for ten to fifteen minutes to rest. Boil some salted water in a big saucepan, and drop the dough into the boiling water bit by bit, a small spoonful at a time. You can use a teaspoon to do this, although in Hungary we had two different kinds of special instruments—a little board on which we put a small amount of dough and then cut it into tiny pieces with a small knife, and a colander-type strainer, through which we pressed the dough with a wooden spoon. The little dumplings should be boiled for ten to twelve minutes—the exact time depends on their size—and then drained. Lastly melt a piece of lard or butter in another saucepan, put in the nockerli, mix well, and serve very hot.

Dumpling   Another kind of dumpling can be made with exactly the same dough mixed with cubes of bread. Cut white bread or rolls into very small cubes, put them in a well-greased baking tin, and heat in the oven until golden-brown and very crisp. Mix these with the dough—which can be just a shade softer than for nockerli—and then, with wet hands, fashion the mixture into dumplings about the size of tennis balls. Drop these into boiling salted water, and boil for about twenty to twenty-five minutes. Drain, and put in a greased dish.

We used these dumplings with all sorts of game, especially hare and venison, and with ox tongue with a brown sauce. They can be served with any meat that has a good sauce, which they need very much. If you like you can add onions to the list of ingredients for these dumplings. Chop them finely, sauté until a golden colour, and then mix into the dough at the same time as the crisp bread-cubes.

These dumplings are very large, like big balls, if they are well made, and very tasty too; although in restaurants they are often stodgy. My elder son liked these dumplings very much as a boy. They were popular in Austria as well as Hungary, and when we were there once on a summer holiday they served them with sour meat and sauce. My son George did not care for the meat, but he ate the dumplings without stopping—and when he had finished he asked for more. I said, "No, you will be sick." However, the kind waitress brought him two more. I said, "You can have them later, but not now." We were sharing a bed-room with my son, and I woke in the middle of the night hearing a noise. On investigating I found my dear little son eating a cold, hard dumpling very happily. He was not taken ill.

A very good *Rolled Dumpling* can be made with potato dough. Boil the potatoes in their jackets, skin them, and press them through a sieve. Mix with flour—the amount cannot be given, it is simply as much as the potatoes will take in—and a pinch of salt. Add two whole eggs but no water, and work very quickly or the dough will be too soft. When it is ready, roll it out as thinly as you can on a well-floured board. Roast some white breadcrumbs in plenty of butter until they are a brown colour, and spread them on the rolled-out dough. Roll it up, and then roll it up again like a Chelsea bun. Place it in a large table napkin, tie up the napkin, put in salted boiling water and boil for about half an hour. Take the dumpling out of the napkin, put it in a hot buttered dish, and serve with hot browned butter.

Rolled Dumpling

A Russian speciality is *Piroshki*, which I tasted first in the home of a Russian family in Berlin. They were among the very first refugees who fled from Russia after the Revolution. Many went to Berlin then, and beautiful ladies of the aristocracy became shop assistants and waitresses,

Piroshki (Three Recipes)

while the men got jobs as taxi-drivers and coachmen. A few managed to salvage some money or jewels, and several of these used their capital to open restaurants in Berlin. I became friendly with one of these families, and they introduced me to both bortsch and piroshki.

The piroshkis I ate at this house were made with a rich choux paste and filled with a mixture of chopped veal, chopped ham, egg, cream, salt, and black pepper. To make the choux paste, boil six ounces of butter in half a pint of water with a little sugar and a little salt. When it is boiling vigorously, add six ounces of flour, mixing it in with a wooden spoon. It is essential that this paste should be well cooked. Allow to cool for a short while, then add five eggs, one by one, beating each one in well before adding the next. Finally pipe the paste on to trays and bake in a warm oven. This choux paste can be used for eclairs or buns as well as piroshkis, which should look like small eclairs.

Any savoury mixture can be used for the filling— chopped meat, ham, egg, mushroom, onion, and so on. When you have filled the piroshkis, cover them with a Béchamel sauce (see page 117), roll them in very fine breadcrumbs, and fry in very hot fat or oil.

II   Another way of making piroshkis is with puff pastry (see page 171). Roll it out very thinly, and cut it into small square pieces. The best filling is cream cheese, which should be mixed with one or two egg-yolks, a little cream, salt, paprika, and chopped dill or chopped chives. Put a teaspoonful on each square and fold it to make a triangle, then brush over with egg-yolk and let it rest for an hour. Brush over again with egg-yolk, put a little grated Parmesan cheese on each piroshki, and bake in a moderate oven.

III   I have also had piroshkis made with shortbread pastry. This is made of flour, one or two eggs, a little white wine, a piece of butter, and a little salt. Mix well, and roll out very thinly. Then add the filling. A good one for this type of piroshki is a mixture of half a pound of minced veal, a quarter of a pound of chopped ham, a whole egg, some fresh cream, one small onion, chopped and sautéd with three or four chopped mushrooms, and salt and black pepper. You need enough cream to make it possible to spread the filling on the shortbread as thickly as possible. When this is done, roll up the pastry, brush over with egg-yolk, let it rest for an hour or so, and bake in a moderate oven for about an hour and a quarter, or until golden-brown. You can serve this sliced very thinly, either cold or hot.

Couscous is a famous North African dish, of which there are some variations as different ingredients are used in Morocco and Algeria. In Morocco I had it made of semolina, but you can use millet instead. I think the Arabs make it from all kinds of grain husk or corn.

Couscous

You need special utensils for it. You must have an earthenware saucepan and an earthenware strainer that has to fit on the saucepan. First boil some dried brown beans in salted water in the saucepan. In another pot put the semolina or millet, or whatever it is you use, and pour boiling water on it, just enough to make it wet when you let it stand for half an hour, and stir. When it has swelled enough, add some olive oil and put it in the strainer, then put the strainer on the earthenware pan in which the beans are cooking. Cover the top of the strainer with a cloth, and let the beans simmer, and steam semolina, for three hours. When no more steam comes out mix the two. The dish is ready.

Instead of beans you can use mutton or chicken or lamb. If you use meat, brown it first with oil, with some onions, carrots, haricot beans, green peas, and pimentos, season well, add water, and then put the strainer on with the semolina and carry on in the same way. When it is done, make a sauce with a little stock and butter and plenty of seasoning, put the meat and vegetables on a hot round dish surrounded by the semolina, and pour the sauce on it.

CHAPTER THIRTEEN

BREAD AND OTHER YEAST DOUGHS

I LIKE bread more than any other food. I could easily live on bread and butter—provided I had a great variety of bread and a really good tasty butter. I mean butter that tastes like butter, and that is not always easy to get.

I choose my bread according to the time of the day, my appetite, and my mood. If my appetite and mood are good I like a light white roll or white bread for breakfast, and of course hot white toast. I nearly always love a slice of hard rye bread with butter for my eleven o'clock coffee. With lunch I like a very crisp Kaiser roll, and with afternoon tea a croissant or brioche. On the dinner table I may have white bread, rolls, French bread, wholemeal bread, or the famous and very popular granary bread.

It is easy as well as delightful to have different breads, not just on a single day but for every day. In a good baker's shop nowadays you can find an enormous variety of bread, and it is worth while to go through them all at least once, if only to find out which ones you like best.

Of course nothing can replace the joy of home-made bread, and the very thought of it brings back memories fragrant with the heavenly, heavenly smell of the freshly baked bread of my childhood. Tuesday was our bread-making day, and I loved it just as I hated Friday, when the cleaning of the house (bad enough on any day) was even fiercer than during the rest of the week. But bread-making began on Monday evening.

148

A large, cradle-shaped wooden bowl was brought into the kitchen. It was spotlessly clean, having been thoroughly scrubbed before being put away and again before use—happy, leisurely days! The flour was sieved into the bowl and pushed to one side. In the other end of the bowl the preliminary small dough—a little flour, a few ounces of yeast, a pinch of salt, and a little luke-warm water—was mixed together. Then the bowl was covered with a large, snow-white cloth, and on top of it a special white blanket was placed; and it was left in a warm place for the night.

The night was very short for the cook and the housewife. At five o'clock in the morning the bowl was uncovered, and the rest of the flour, with more salt and lukewarm water, was kneaded together. Finally the bread was baked in a special oven which looked like a big, overgrown balloon. It was lovely to sit round on cold, winter days, as it gave a very pleasant heat. It was heated with wood, and every cook or housewife knew how to use it and how to get the right temperature, without having to use a thermometer, let alone thermostatic apparatus. And I never remember seeing a burnt loaf, and certainly not an under-baked one.

The flour varied each time we made bread. Sometimes it was snow-white, sometimes snow-white with potatoes. The next time carraway seed was added, then brown wheat flour was used. Another week, perhaps, rye flour with bran and hops were mixed together. Sometimes a very unusual flavour was added to the flour: the golden outside leaves of large onions were put into warm water and soaked for ten minutes, and the water was used in the bread-making, giving the bread a very good flavour with a soupçon of onions. Each of these breads had a different smell—and each smell was beautiful and delicious. For that reason, I think, bread-making is one of the happiest of my happy childhood memories.

If you are lucky enough to have the time—and it would be misleading to pretend you don't need it—why not give your family the pleasure of home-made bread? Nowadays you can get all kinds of flour from grocery shops, and wholemeal and special rye flours in health shops, so there is plenty of scope. In this chapter I am going to suggest several recipes, drawn mostly from my childhood. In some cases you will probably find the quantities too large; when that happens, just scale them down in proportion, dividing by two or three or whatever you like. But don't scale them down too much, for when you go to the trouble to make bread you will want to see enough produced—and, of course, consumed—to make you feel it was worth while.

Standard Household Bread (Two Recipes) Let's begin with *Standard Household Bread*.

Mix three and a half pounds of flour with one and a quarter ounces of salt. Rub in two ounces of fat. Dissolve two ounces of yeast in one and a half pints of warm water, add to the dry ingredients, and mix to a firm dough. Allow to stand for one hour, and then knock it back—that is, press on the dough until all the gas has been pushed out, to enable the yeast still active in the dough to begin working afresh. Wait a further quarter of an hour, then divide into pieces and mould into shapes. Bake at a temperature of 450°F.

II Another household bread:

Three pounds of white flour and a tablespoon of salt, mixed with an ounce of yeast dissolved in one and three-quarters pints of lukewarm water. Knead until smooth and silky, cover with a cloth and a blanket, keep in a warm place and let it rise for about one or one and a half hours. Put it on a well-floured board and shape three loaves out of it. Put in greased bread-tins and allow to rise for another half an hour, then bake at about 350°F.

Rye Bread (Two Recipes) Now *Rye Bread*. Mix two pounds of rye flour, one pound of white flour, and one and a half ounces of salt in a bowl in a warm place. Dissolve an ounce of yeast in a quarter of a pint of water, add a very little sugar and a little flour, and mix to a dough. Leave this yeast dough to rise until it cracks on top, then mix with the flour and half a pint of water, and knead until smooth and silky. According to the old saying, you go on working it with your hands until they are clean from the dough. Now cover the dough with a tea-cloth and a big blanket, and let it rise for an hour or more, until it comes to the top of the bowl. When it has risen, push it back into the bowl and let it rise another half an hour. Then place the dough on a floured board and make two loaves from it, and put them in bread tins greased with unflavoured (preferably vegetable) fat. Cover up again, and leave to rest for another half-hour; then place in the oven at 350°F. Test when firm and sound, and then the bread is ready.

Alternatively you can make ryebread with sour dough. *II* This time use one and a half pounds of rye flour and a pound of white flour. To make the sour dough, mix four or five ounces of the mixed flour with a little warm water and a pinch of sugar, and put it aside for three or four days or even longer. Add this and a tablespoon of salt to the rest of the flour mixture, some caraway seed if you like, a pinch of sugar, and three-quarters of a pint of warm water. The water should be really warm. Work with the hands till they are clean from the dough, and then continue as in the first recipe for rye bread. Before baking you should take four or five ounces from the dough and keep it for sour dough for the next time.

When I was in Denmark I went over an interesting bread factory, which produced a special Danish bread that takes twenty-four hours to make. The factory was owned by all the small bakeries and run on a sort of co-operative and profit-sharing basis. It was an excellent bakery, making the most wonderful bread. Some of it was sliced and wrapped in tinfoil ready for distribution.

If you want to make *Danish Rye Bread*, put one pound *Danish* of fine ryemeal with half an ounce of yeast, two ounces of *Rye Bread* sugar, and two pints of water into a bowl, and leave in a warm place until sour. Add half a pound of white flour, half a pound of fine ryemeal, and one ounce of salt, and knead to a firm dough. Mould into one-pound pieces, and put in a baking tin. As this is a sour dough recipe, the final proof will take rather longer than ordinary bread. It must be baked slowly and well at 380°F.

A few years ago I was in Düsseldorf at the time of the International Bakery Exhibition, and there were some very good displays of bread and pastries. The German exhibits were the best—artistic and meticulously precise, and often exquisitely elaborate. Their equipment was of excellent workmanship. I saw the most modern ovens—four storeys high, very up-to-date, and easily cleaned. I would have liked to buy a number of things for my own bakery, but Customs difficulties prevented me.

Austrian   Among the exhibits was *Austrian Rye Bread*, for which
Rye Bread   you need not the ryemeal that you use for Danish rye bread but fine rye flour. Put half a pound of this with half a pound of white flour into a bowl with two ounces of sugar and one and a half pints of warm water, and leave to stand in a warm place for twenty-four hours. When sour, add one pound of white flour, two pounds of fine rye flour, two ounces of salt, two ounces of finely ground carraway seeds, three-quarters of an ounce of yeast, and enough warm water to make into a smooth, firm dough. This type of bread is moulded into round pieces and proved in small, well-greased cane baskets, then turned out on to baking sheets and baked slowly and well.

At home I liked the rye bread the best of all. On the other hand, the days when the white bread was made were more exciting, because then breakfast was an additional joy. We got hot langosh, which was something like a thick pancake made of bread dough and baked on the top of the wood-heated oven which acted as your hot-plate acts to-day. Langosh with fresh butter was really a delicacy, and thrilled us all. So did the special loaf made for us children from the dough that came off the bottom of the wooden bread bowl when Cook scrubbed it before putting it away. She made this dough into a tiny loaf—or perhaps into the

shape of a little bird with two peppercorns for eyes—for us
children to eat at lunch-time. It was a little hard but very
crisp, and we loved it.

On my way to school I used to pass a delicatessen shop,
where my father opened an account for me. I was allowed
to have a roll every day with any of the enormous variety
of sausages that this shop had. Each time it was a problem
to decide which slices I should ask to be put into my roll.
Now the school to which I went every day also had
boarders, and for their "elevenses" the boarders were
given a slice of plain brown rye bread. The nuns who ran
the school made this bread—and it was so wonderful that
all of us day-girls, who came with rolls with butter and
sausage, wanted to swap with the boarders. We were not
always successful.

We had another great pleasure at school. At the ten
o'clock break, which was the longest, we went out into the
yard, where an old lady with a huge basket sold huge
pretzels, which were crisp, salty, and just wonderful. I
don't think that anything has ever had such a good flavour
as those *Pretzels*, and they cost about one-sixth of a penny   *Pretzels*
each. Here is the recipe—although I cannot promise quite
the same flavour of the pretzels the old lady sold in the
school yard.

You want two and half pounds of flour, a little salt, an
ounce of yeast, and enough water to make the dough very
firm. Knead it well, and then divide into small balls, as
many as you want to make. Pretzels may be as much as
seven or eight inches in diameter, or as little as three.
Roll out the little balls in long strips like thick cord, and
shape them like pretzels. Then leave them to rest in a
warm place for thirty or thirty-five minutes. Boil some
water in a large shallow pan, and drop the pretzels into
the water one by one. Let them boil for eight to ten
minutes, take each out very carefully so as not to spoil the
shape, and drop them into cold water. Take them out and
put them on a dry tea cloth, and leave for a few minutes

to dry. Place them on a baking sheet and bake in a moderate oven till crisp and golden-brown. In the meantime mix salt with a little flour and water for a paste, and spread this gently on the pretzels after they are baked. Leave to dry. If you like you can put the salted pretzels back in the oven to dry them more quickly—they need only a minute. It may sound a lot of fussing about, but the result can be a delight for every child.

Honey Bran Bread   One of the best yeast doughs for home baking is *Honey Bran Bread*. For this you need (halve the quantities if you like) five and a half pounds of white flour and two and a half pounds of wholemeal flour, two ounces of malt, four ounces of bran, four ounces of honey, three and a half ounces of salt and the same amount of yeast, and a pint and a quarter of water. Mix the flours, malt, bran, and salt thoroughly in their dry state. Dissolve the honey in part of the water, and add to the mixture. Finally dissolve the yeast in the rest of the water and add slowly. Mix until a dough of smooth texture is achieved. Leave it to rise for an hour, mould to any shape, allow to rise again for twenty-five to thirty minutes in a warm place, and bake at 450°F.

Potato Bread   To make *Potato Bread*, mix together two pounds of high-protein flour, six ounces of finely mashed potatoes, one ounce of salt, half an ounce of sugar, and one ounce of fat. Dissolve one and a half ounces of yeast in four-fifths of a pint of water, and add slowly until you get a firm, smooth dough. After one hour's proving, knock the dough back and then shape into loaves weighing about one pound each. Prove again for twenty minutes, and then bake in a hot oven at 450°F. Before baking, the bread should be cut crossways on the top and dusted with a little flour.

At home for special occasions we used to make rolls, crescents, and long batons, with salt and carraway seeds on top. For these we added some butter and milk in the dough. In Hungary we had several bread rolls that are not *Kaiser Rolls*   made here. One was the famous *Kaiser Rolls* which my bakery makes now. Here is the recipe.

Mix together two and a half pounds of flour, a quarter of an ounce of malt, three-quarters of an ounce of salt, half an ounce of sugar, and one and a quarter ounces of butter in their dry state, then add one-third of a pint of milk. Dissolve one and a quarter ounces of yeast in half a pint of water, add, and mix the dough to a smooth texture. Cut it up into one-ounce pieces, and mould and cut each into the characteristic Kaiser shape. This used to be done by hand. Each piece was moulded into a round shape, and then you chopped it with the edge of your hand and folded in, and did this all the way round. Today you can get a cutter with a spindle held in the handle, so that as the cutter is pressed into the piece of dough it turns and folds one cut over the next. After moulding, leave to prove for twenty minutes, then bake at 450°F. for twenty-five to thirty minutes.

Another bread roll that was popular in Hungary was the *Water Semmel*, which was very crisp, very light, and just a little sour to taste.

Water Semmel

Mix two and a half pounds of strong Canadian or Hungarian flour with half an ounce of butter, half an ounce of sugar, and an ounce of salt, and add half a pint of warm water. Dissolve one and a quarter ounces of yeast in two-thirds of a pint of water, and mix until a smooth, firm dough is formed. Allow this dough to rest in a warm place for three hours, and then remould it. Finally divide into two-ounce pieces, mould them round, and allow to prove for thirty minutes. Bake in an oven at 450°F.

For *Butter Malt Sticks* you need two pounds of flour, an ounce of yeast, two-thirds of an ounce of salt, one ounce of Diamalt—a malt product, a kind of baking powder which improves the dough—one ounce of butter, two and one-third ounces of olive oil. Make a paste of rather solid consistency of all the ingredients. Let it rise twice, and beat it down twice. Shape into long sticks, prove and then bake in about 450°F.

Butter Malt Sticks

For *Milk Bread Rolls* you need two pounds of flour, five

Milk Bread Rolls

ounces of butter, one ounce of yeast, two eggs, one third
of a pint of fresh milk with one third of a pint of warm
water, three-quarters of an ounce of salt, and one ounce of
malt. Make a softish dough with ten ounces of the flour,
some cool liquid, and yeast, and work it well. Add the
rest of the ingredients, and leave to rise in a cool place
overnight. Next morning work it well, and leave to rise
again, after forming rolls which should be covered by a
cloth. With a thin rolling pin press down the centres of the
rolls and put into a cool room. Put in trays, and bake in a
moderate oven for twenty to twenty-five minutes.

Light Dinner   For *Light Dinner Rolls* mix together five pounds of
Rolls   high-protein flour, three and a half ounces of butter, and
one and three-quarters of an ounce of salt in their dry state.
Dissolve one and three-quarters of an ounce of yeast in
two and a quarter pints of water, and add slowly. Continue
mixing until a smooth dough is achieved. Bake in a
moderate oven. (Reduce quantities proportionately if you
want to make less.)

Croissants   For croissants you need two pounds of flour, one pound
of butter, three quarters of a pint of milk, two ounces of
yeast, two ounces of sugar, quarter of an ounce of salt
and six eggs. First mix together half your milk with six
ounces of the flour and the yeast and leave this to stand
in a warm place for half an hour. Now take the rest of the
flour, add half a pound of the butter, the sugar, the salt
and eggs. Mix this to a dough with the rest of the milk.
Blend the two doughs and allow to stand for an hour.
After this roll it out and place the rest of the butter over
one half of the dough and then fold it over. Roll and fold
over again. Then place in the refrigerator until firm.
Then roll it out into a long strip, cut into triangles and
roll up from the wide end. Put them on a baking sheet,
allow to rise, brush with egg and bake in a moderate
oven for about twenty-five minutes.

The other favourite French breakfast food is the
Brioche   delicate, elegant, and light *Brioche*, which, if well made,

starts the day in the most joyful way. It is just as pleasant in the afternoon, and especially good with a cup of choco-late. Here is the recipe.

Take eight ounces of flour, and put one-quarter of this in a small bowl; then in the middle of it put about a quarter of an ounce of yeast and a quarter of a pint of lukewarm milk. Let the yeast dissolve, and work in the flour. Put the resulting dough aside and leave it for about half an hour to rise. Now in another, bigger bowl put the rest of the flour, two whole eggs and an extra egg-yolk, and start to knead with your hands, beating vigorously to give the dough elasticity. Keep two and a half ounces of butter handy, in a warm place, and slowly add this to the dough. Also add a pinch of salt, a tablespoon of sugar, and the grated peel of one lemon.

When the dough containing the yeast has risen, beat it and then mix it with the second dough, and work the mix-ture with your hands till it leaves them clean. Let it stand in a warm place for about an hour and a half—until it has risen to about double its original size. Then beat it down—this should break the dough—and leave it in a cold place for about half an hour.

Grease the little brioche moulds with butter, and from the dough make little round balls. From each of these pull out a piece of dough but don't break it; just make a knob on top of the ball, to give the brioche its characteristic shape. Leave to rise again for about fifteen minutes, then brush the balls over with egg-yolk. Put in the greased moulds, and bake in a moderate oven for about twenty-five minutes.

Savoury or salty brioche is made in the same way, only you need more salt and only very little sugar, and instead of milk you can use lukewarm water.

Similar ingredients are used to make *Kugloph*, which I *Kugloph* think originated in Vienna; certainly it is widely associated with the famous Viennese coffee which always has wonder-ful whipped cream on top. But it was a favourite with coffee in Hungary too, and indeed all over Eastern Europe. You can make it in many forms. The Hungarian mould that I use is shaped exactly the same as the Austrian mould. The Russians, who also had kugloph, used to make it—I don't know what they do now—in a different shape, rather like a mitre, and they poured fondant (see page 166) on top of it after it was baked.

As for the brioche, take eight ounces of flour and begin by making a ferment with a little of this and half an ounce of yeast and a little milk. Leave to rise in a warm place. Put the rest of the flour in a large mixing bowl, and add the first dough, then three or four eggs one by one, three and a half ounces of softened butter little by little, some well-washed sultanas, an ounce of sugar and a pinch of salt, and as much lukewarm milk as the flour will take. This dough also must be elastic, so knead well with your hands. Again, it will be ready when the dough no longer clings to your hands. Let it rise until nearly double its original size, then make it into a big round ball and put it in a well-buttered special kugloph mould. Let it rise for another twenty-five to thirty minutes, then bake in a moderate oven.

Golden   Another member of the wide yeast-dough family is
Galushka   *Golden Galushka*, a glorified bun dough. To make this, first dissolve an ounce of yeast in a little milk and very little flour, and let it rise for a few minutes. Then add five egg-yolks, four ounces of butter, a tablespoon of sugar, a pinch of salt and one pound ten ounces of flour. Mix all together with enough milk to make a soft dough. Work it till you get little bubbles in the dough, then put it in a warm place and let it rise. In the meantime take about one pound of walnuts and the same amount of sugar, and pound them in a mortar; leave it quite coarse—it should not be fine. Add some sultanas to this mixture if you like, and put it into a bowl. Melt half a pound of butter, and put this into another bowl. When the dough has risen nicely, put it on a floured board and take very small pieces, each about the size of a walnut, and drop them first in the warm butter and then in the sugared walnut, one by one; and finally

drop them in a deep baking tin that you have buttered well and sprinkled with chopped walnuts. Continue until the tin is three-quarters full. Then leave for twenty minutes or so for the dough to rise again, and bake in a moderate oven for about an hour. Serve hot with a wine sauce, rum sauce, or vanilla sauce, according to taste.

Another luxury cake made with yeast is *Beigle*, the Hungarian Christmas cake—which in fact was eaten at any festive occasion just like the English fruit cake. Mix together one pound three ounces of flour, four ounces of sugar, a little salt, and five ounces of butter. Add six egg-yolks, as much milk as the flour will take up—but it shouldn't be soft—and two ounces of yeast dissolved in a little milk. Work together well, and leave to rest for an hour.

Beigle

For the filling you need one pound of ground walnuts, eight ounces of sugar, four ounces of honey, seven ounces of finely chopped orange peel, seven ounces of sultanas, the grated peel of one lemon, and a little cinnamon. Boil all these together with a little milk—enough to enable you to stir the mixture without making it soft. Let it cool.

Weigh one pound of dough and one pound of the mixture for the filling. Roll out the dough very thinly, and spread the filling on it; the rolled-out dough should be the same thickness as the filling. Roll in together, making a long shape or a large crescent. Let it rest for half an hour, then brush it with egg-yolk; let it rest another fifteen minutes, then brush again with egg-yolk; let it rest another fifteen minutes, then brush finally with egg-yolk to which a little sugar has been added, to give the Beigle a nice brown colour after baking. It is best to leave the rolled-up Beigle in the refrigerator or some other very cold place overnight. Bake in a moderate oven for an hour or so.

Here is another *Christmas Beigle*.

Christmas Beigle

The ingredients for the dough are two pounds four ounces of flour, two pounds two ounces of butter, three and half ounces of sugar, an ounce and a half of yeast, six ounces of milk, six egg-yolks, a little salt and a little rum. Mix well together, and leave to rest for an hour.

For the filling you need one pound eight ounces of ground walnuts, two pounds of sugar, three-quarters of a pint of milk, four ounces of lemon peel, six ounces of sultanas, and eight ounces of cake-crumbs. Boil all these together—again, the mixture should not be too soft. Let it cool, and then fill the dough and continue in exactly the same way as for the first Christmas Beigle.

Poppy-seed Beigle is made in exactly the same way as Walnut Beigle: in either recipe just substitute poppy-seeds for ground walnuts.

Pité   Ground walnuts or poppy-seeds, again, are good for filling another Hungarian speciality, what I might call our everyday luncheon pastry, known as *Pité*. It was always the same and always different—that is, same pastry, different filling.

The ingredients for the pastry are ten ounces of fresh butter, twice that amount of flour, three egg-yolks, a pinch of salt, two or three tablespoons of thick cream— enough to make the pastry not too soft and not too hard— and a little white wine or rum and a little sugar. Work until smooth, and leave in a cold place to rest for an hour or so. Then take half the pastry, roll it out, and place it in a baking tin. Prick it with a fork. Put it in a medium-hot oven, and bake until half done. Take it out of the oven and brush it over with apricot jam (or any other jam you like).

Apple Pité   Now if it is going to be an *Apple Pité*, for example, you need to make an apple purée. For this, core and peel some cooking apples, and cook them with very little water, some grated lemon peel, a few sultanas, and sugar. When the purée is cool, put it on the pastry in the baking tin and, if you like, sprinkle a little powdered cinnamon on the apple. Now roll out the other half of the pastry, and cover the apple with it. Brush it with egg-yolk mixed with a little sugar, make some nice decorative marks with a fork, and bake brown.

Other fillings can be made with fruits in season. To make the filling for *Cherry Pité*, for example, stone some cherries and mix them with a little cinnamon and sugar. For *Redcurrant Pité*, simply put redcurrants on the dough in the baking tin and sprinkle with sugar. In this case, however, you do not cover the filling with a dough, but put on it very stiffly beaten and sugared egg-whites and then bake till the top is brown.

Cherry or Red-currant Pité

In *Cream Cheese Pité* also the pastry is only underneath. To make the filling for this, pass six or seven ounces of cream cheese through a sieve, mix well with three or four egg-yolks and sugar according to your taste, and add four to eight tablespoons of thick cream. Whisk the whites of the eggs very stiffly, mix in, and again taste for sugar— the filling should be pleasantly sweet. Add the grated peel of one lemon and a few well-washed sultanas. Mix very gently, taking care not to break the egg-white. Pour the mixture on the dough, and bake in a moderate oven for about an hour.

Cream Cheese Pité

Hungarian Doughnuts have no connection—except in name—with English, American, or even Austrian dough-nuts. They are big, very light, and delicious. Several of my women friends would eat seven or eight of them after a big dinner. We used to eat them especially on New Year's Eve, at exactly twelve o'clock—a custom that has been adopted by other countries, Germany and Austria in particular, but which is truly Hungarian in origin.

Hungarian Doughnuts

The measurements of the ingredients must be exact. You need one pound and three ounces of plain flour; one ounce of yeast; three ounces of butter; two ounces of sugar; eight egg-yolks; the grated peel of one lemon; a pinch of salt; half a liqueur glass of very good rum; three pounds of pure lard; and half a pint of lukewarm milk.

Take about two ounces of the flour and add to the yeast with a quarter of a pint of the lukewarm milk, a little of the sugar, and a pinch of salt. Mix together, put in a warm place, and allow to rise. When the dough has risen, mix it with all the remaining ingredients, with the exception of the lard, work to a moderately soft dough, and then completely cover the bowl and allow to rise. This will take a good hour. Now place this dough on a well-floured board, and roll out a quarter of an inch thick. Cut into round shapes, using a one-and-a-half-inch cutter. Allow a further twenty minutes for rising.

Melt the lard in a deep frier, and when it is very hot drop in the doughnuts and cover with a lid for a few minutes. Turn the doughnuts, and leave until golden-brown. You can tell when they are well made by a pale rim that appears in the middle. They should, of course, be as light as a feather.

From doughnuts we used to make a savoury dish for shooting parties. They were filled with ham and served with tomato sauce.

CHAPTER FOURTEEN

CAKES AND PASTRIES

My father died when I was young, and that was the first terrible shock and tragedy in my life. The second was my mother's death, which occurred when I was already married and had two children. Her passing left a big blank in my life. I had always seen my mother every day, and in her last illness often two or three times a day. She used to complain, "You are with me so little"; and when I said, "But, Mother, I am so often here," she would answer, "Often, but not enough." After she died I went every Sunday to the cemetery, and I came home feeling more and more empty for having lost her. After a few months I decided that these visits were no good to her or to me. It was then that I decided I would find some work to do.

The obvious thing was to go into my husband's business, especially as it was the kind of business in which a woman could be helpful. I decided to give myself three months to discover whether I was fit to be a business-woman. When the three months ended I never even noticed it, for I had made the discovery that the best cure for everything sad in life is to do something—to escape to work. Nothing I know has helped me more. From the beginning the work interested and amused me, and it has done ever since.

The factory had three departments. These were the chocolate-making, the pastry-making—which always went by the name of the bakery—and the box-making. At first I just learnt everything that was happening, going in at the beginning of the day's work and not leaving until the factory closed in the evening. Eventually I decided to take over the bakery, which was in a separate building. And that was how my present career began.

The competition in Budapest was extremely keen, and overshadowing all our rivals—and us, at first—was the world-famous Gerbeaud. The Hungarian public was always difficult to please, and it is characteristic that for decades Gerbeaud's bonbons were the only ones a gentleman would think of sending as a present to a lady. So it was a great achievement when, after a few years, Floris chocolates became considered equally permissible as a gift.

Floris gateaux and pastries had to fight equally hard for their equality. One of Gerbeaud's most famous pastries was the mignon, and it was so popularly associated with him that the general public called it only Gerbeaud, in the same way as some of you say Player's instead of cigarettes. Often it happened that people would come to *our* shop and ask for Gerbeauds instead of mignons!

Now, I think, I could write a whole book on mignons, or petit fours. If you want to make a really decorative tea-table, with a variety of small but delicious pastries, try

Mignons   these *Mignons*; all you need is time and a lot of patience!

Beat four egg-whites with three and a half ounces of sugar until stiff, then mix carefully with three and a half ounces of ground almonds. With a forcing bag place small rounds on a baking board which has been covered with grease-proof paper. Bake in a very moderate oven for about fifteen or twenty minutes; they must not be hard, but should be kept soft and light. Take them off the board with a knife, and put two together with raspberry jam or a light chocolate cream. Ice with fondant (see page 166)—pink for raspberry jam, chocolate for chocolate cream. That is

(*Mignon*   one sort of mignon.

Bases)   The base for that mignon is what is called *Banny*. There

Banny   are several other mixtures, any of which may be used as a

Pomponette   common base for a variety of mignons. One of the best of these bases is *Pomponette*. For this you need three whole eggs and three more egg-yolks, three and a half ounces of sugar and the same amount of flour. Mix well together, and then pipe in rounds on greaseproof paper. Bake on a board in a moderate oven until they are firm but not hard.

Coki is another good base. The mixture is made with three stiffly beaten egg-whites, two ounces of sugar, a pound of marzipan, and four ounces of flour. Again pipe in rounds on to greaseproof paper. Dust with icing sugar and bake on a board in a moderate oven. Keep them very soft and light. *Coki*

Then there is *Déak* mixture, for which you need eight egg-yolks, four ounces of butter, five ounces of flour, eight and a half ounces of sugar, four ounces of ground almonds —and, if you can get them, about five bitter almonds, crushed or grated. Pipe the mixture, in round or oval shapes. Bake on a tray in a moderate oven for fifteen or twenty minutes. *Déak*

So much for mignon bases, each of which allows you to make a variety of mignons.

Cherry Marzipan Mignon is a good one. Soften a pound of marzipan with two ounces of Kirsch liqueur, and pipe in a small circle on the base. Cut glacé cherries into four, and place the pieces in the form of a cross on this ball of marzipan and Kirsch. Glaze with boiled apricot jam, and dip in white fondant. *Cherry Marzipan Mignon*

Then there are *Coffee Chestnut Mignons*, for which you need chestnut paste (see page 170). Soften one pound of this with two ounces of rum, and pipe on to the base. Place pieces of marrons glacés on the ball, glaze with boiled apricot jam, and dip in coffee fondant. *Coffee Chestnut Mignon*

For *Chocolate Hazelnut Praline Mignons* first make half a pound of buttercream and beat this with half a pound of praline until quite smooth. Beat into this two ounces of melted slab chocolate. Pipe the mixture on to the base, and cover with crushed toasted hazelnuts. Glaze with boiled apricot jam, and dip in chocolate fondant. *Chocolate Hazelnut Praline*

White
Fondant

The *Fondant* with which mignons are iced is made with sugar and glucose. Boil two pounds of lump sugar in half a pint of water. When the temperature is 225°F. add five ounces of warm melted glucose. When the temperature reaches 240°F. pour the mixture into a flat-bottomed receptacle. When the temperature is reduced to about 100°F. work the mixture with a wooden spatula or spoon until it is thick and white. Cover it with a damp cloth, and use when required by gently heating over a gas with the addition of a little water.

Coloured
Fondant

That is white fondant; but, of course, one of the things that makes mignons so decorative is the fact that they are of many different colours, and the colour matches the flavour. So the fondant has to be orange-coloured if there is an orange filling, yellow if it is pineapple, pale-green for pistachio, and so on. Use vegetable colours for this purpose, adding a very little of the colour—for a little goes a long way—right at the end of the process of making the fondant. Of course you add chocolate if the flavour is chocolate, and coffee for a coffee-flavoured or chestnut filling.

After icing, decorate the mignons with lots of little coloured bits—half a pistachio nut, small cherries, coffee beans, half a walnut, and so on, according to what is inside. A tray of these mignons looks like a beautiful herbaceous border.

So much for mignons, for which our rival Gerbeaud was so justly famous. I worked very hard to make our cakes and pastries at least as good as his. I was lucky to be able to secure a number of pastrycooks who had been with Gerbeaud for many years; indeed, I got his most important key men to work for me. I learnt much from these men as I watched their work all day long. At the beginning I would not say much, but after a while instructions were asked from me, and it would have been fatal to hesitate. Even the wrong decision was better than indecision.

When I started to work in our factory we had no retail

shops of our own. We only delivered to wholesale customers—shops, hotels, and restaurants. Later we opened
our first shop in Budapest—a lovely, very unusual shop,
more like a beautiful room—and it was a great success.
Later we opened other shops, including Konditoreis where
we served tea and coffee and, eventually, lunches and
dinners.

Year by year our businesses became more and more
successful—artistically and morally. We found our work
satisfying and enjoyable; however, because of the financial
crisis all over the world our business became increasingly
less profitable. Then one day a friend of my husband's
came back from England and tried to persuade him to go
and take his products there. At last, in 1931, we took
this step.

Our first home in England was in York. My husband
had a contract with the wonderful Rowntree works. He
liked his work; he liked the people he worked with; he
liked York. I shared his likes, and enjoyed playing the
hostess to Mr. and Mrs. Seebohm Rowntree. They were
very kind to us, and Mrs. Rowntree often called and took
me for a drive in her car over the Yorkshire moors. On
one of these outings she asked me if there was anything
wrong as I always seemed sad. I told her that nothing was
really the matter, except that I would like to work again.
I said that of all the things I missed in England most the
most important was work. She promised she would talk it
over with her husband, and a few months later my present
little business came about.

But I think it is time I stopped talking about myself and
said something about how Floris cakes are made. As in the
chapter on bread, you may find the quantities larger than
you want: in that case simply reduce them proportionately
to suit your needs.

First, let's make a *Fruit and Fresh Cream Gâteau*. Whip
two eggs with two and a half ounces of sugar until stiff,
and, using a wooden spoon, lightly stir in two and a half

*Fruit and
Fresh Cream
Gâteau*

ounces of sieved plain flour. Finally, melt one ounce of
butter and stir this very lightly but thoroughly. Turn the
mixture out into a greased sponge tin, and bake in a
moderate oven (370°F.). When cooked, turn out on a
wire cake tray and allow to cool. When thoroughly cold,
cut the sponge in two and on the bottom half spread a layer
(about a quarter of an inch thick) of fresh whipped cream,
slightly sweetened. On this cream place an assortment of
well-drained tinned fruits. Then spread on another layer
of cream, and finally replace the top half of the sponge.
Coat the top and sides of the sponge with a thin layer of
whipped fresh cream, and place some toasted flaked nuts
round the side. On the top place fruit in various designs,
and slightly glaze this with some warmed and sieved
apricot jam. The gâteau can then be finished off by piping
a little fresh cream round the fruit on the top to make it
very attractive.

Princess A good light almond cake is *Princess Anne Cake*. For
Anne Cake this, take a quarter of a pound of sugar and four egg-yolks,
mix very well, then add two ounces of ground almonds
and one whole egg. Mix until very smooth and creamy.
Now whip up four egg-whites until very stiff, so stiff that
when you turn the bowl upside down they cannot or should
not fall out. Very slowly and lightly mix in two and three-
quarter ounces of flour, and three and a half ounces of
melted butter. Bake in a buttered and floured cake-tin in a
moderate oven (370°F.) for thirty to thirty-five minutes.
When cool, slice the cake into three layers and fill with a
cream filling, which is made as follows :

Pound three and a half ounces of almonds and three and
a half ounces of sugar very finely in a mortar. Then mix
with two and three-quarter ounces of melted butter and the
same amount of melted chocolate. After filling, place the
layers on top of each other, then coat the cake all over with
thick apricot jam and ice with white fondant. If the fondant
worries you, make a praline topping instead. For this,
lightly brown one and a half ounces of almonds in the oven,

then heat two ounces of sugar in a saucepan until light brown in colour, stirring all the time. When all the sugar has melted, stir in the toasted almonds, and place on a greased plate to cool. When hard, place in a mortar and pound into fine crumbs. Spread on the whole cake.

For *Orange Cake*, put a quarter of a pound of caster sugar in a bowl with the grated peel of one orange and four egg-yolks, and whisk until white and creamy. Carefully mix in one and three-quarter ounces of flour and the same amount of potato flour, and at the same time four very stiffly beaten egg-whites. Be very careful with this mixing, or the lightness of the orange cake may be spoilt. Bake in a slow oven in a round tin, buttered and floured, for thirty-five to forty minutes.

Orange Cake

For a *Chocolate Sponge*, whip two eggs with two and a half ounces of sugar until stiff. Thoroughly sieve together two and a half ounces of flour and half an ounce of cocoa powder, and, with a wooden spoon, stir into the whipped eggs and sugar. Finally stir in one ounce of melted butter. Turn the mixture into a greased sponge tin, and bake in a moderate oven (375°F.). When cold, cut the cake in two.

Chocolate Sponge

Partly whip four ounces of fresh cream, and add this to two ounces of melted chocolate. Mix thoroughly. Sandwich the sponge (when cool) with a layer of this cream, and replace the top sponge. Finally coat the sponge top and sides with a thin layer of chocolate cream, and place toasted nuts round the sides. Put some of the cream into a piping bag, and pipe the top of the gâteau with various designs. The decoration can be made more elaborate with the use of nuts.

To make *Mont Blanc*, whip two egg-whites with half an ounce of sugar until stiff. Slowly stir in another three and a half ounces of granulated sugar. Take a sheet of greaseproof paper, and draw on it a circle with a diameter of five inches. Using a plain tube, pipe the meringue into this circle, starting at the centre and working outward. On the outer edge build up with blobs of meringue. Lightly

Mont Blanc

dust this with granulated sugar, and place in a very cool oven to dry out. When dry and firm, pipe into the centre a thick layer of whipped cream and add pieces of crumbled marrons glacés. Take some chestnut purée—which you can buy in tins—and add a little ground almond until a soft paste is formed. Place this into a piping tube, and pipe across the cream in various designs. A little piped whipped cream can also be used to elaborate the design.

Chestnut
Purée

If you like you can, of course, make the *Chestnut Purée* yourself. Take two and a quarter pounds of chestnuts, cut the skins a little with a sharp knife, and drop them into boiling water. Let them boil just a few minutes, long enough so that you can take off the outside hard skin and the brown skin inside. When you have peeled them, put them in a pint and a quarter of milk together with nine or ten ounces of sugar and a small piece of vanilla pod, and boil until the chestnuts are tender. Boil out all the liquid, then pass through a sieve, potato-presser, or forcing-bag with a star-shaped tube. If you like, flavour with rum or any other liqueur.

Walnut
Gâteau

For *Walnut Gâteau*, whip together twelve eggs and twelve egg-yolks with eleven ounces of sugar; blend in seven ounces of ground walnuts, four and a half ounces of flour, a pinch of cinnamon, and the grated rind of a lemon; and finally fold in three ounces of melted butter. Bake in a shallow round tin in a hot oven. When cold, fill with a cream made of two ounces of sugar, two ounces of butter, and one ounce of ground walnuts. Edge with toasted walnuts, and cover the top with coffee fondant (see page 166). Complete the decorations with walnuts and caramel sugar (sugar melted to a light-brown colour).

Boy Friend
Gâteau

To make *Boy Friend Gâteau* beat five egg-yolks with one ounce of sugar and blend with five whites which have been beaten stiff with two ounces of sugar. Finally fold in two ounces of ground hazelnuts, two ounces of ground walnuts and half an ounce of grated chocolate. Place in greased floured hoops and bake at a temperature of 380°F.

When cold, layer with coffee butter cream mixed with crushed nougatine. Cover the top with coffee fondant icing and edge with toasted flaked almonds. Place half walnuts round the top edge of the cake and decorate with caramel sugar.

For *Linzer Gâteau* you need unblanched almonds— thirteen ounces of them, which you grate and then mix with the same amount of butter and the same of sugar, one pound two ounces of flour, two whole eggs, one egg-yolk, a pinch of cinnamon, and half a glass of milk. Work together lightly until smooth and silky, and roll out half the dough to a thickness of half an inch. Put it in a flan case, and spread with apricot or raspberry jam. Roll out the other half of the dough into long round strips, and put these criss-cross on the jam. Brush over with egg-yolk and bake in a moderate oven.

Linzer Gâteau

Pischinger is rich and delicious. Layer up toasted sheets of wafer biscuits with layers of praline which has been softened with a little glycerine, making about seven layers in all. When set cut into long bars and cover half with green and half with pink marzipan. With a sharp knife cut the bars into small slices.

Pischinger

For *Hungarian Cream Slice*, place nine egg-yolks with four ounces of sugar and a little milk into a bowl. Bring to the boil two and a half pints of milk with a vanilla pod, add to the egg-yolk mixture, and cook slowly. While still cooking, fold in nine whites of eggs, after whipping them stiffly with ten ounces of sugar. Sandwich thickly between two thin sheets of mille-feuille, and cut into slices.

Hungarian Cream Slice

To come to something more international, there is the very useful and popular *Puff Pastry*. It is easy to make if you keep to the rules—and, of course, the first rule is that you need a lot of patience. The second is that you should have a light hand. You must handle the dough gently; if you don't you will still achieve something, but it will not be puff pastry—rather more like elastic. Another important point is to remember how you have done each

Puff Pastry

folding, because you have to fold the dough several times, and each time in another way. If you can master these few little tricks you will know how to make something that you can use in dozens of ways—for hors-d'oeuvre, for cocktail savouries, for vol-au-vents, and for endless sweets and gâteaux.

To give an exact recipe for puff pastry is difficult. Flour varies in its capacity to absorb liquid, and butter varies in its liquid content, so that precise measurements of these ingredients could be misleading. However, if you have a little feeling for cooking you will soon find the way.

There are a number of different ways of making puff pastry. Here's mine.

Take about half a pound of flour, put it on a board with a little salt, add water and mix a dough very lightly with your finger-tips. You may need half a pint of water, but only use as much as the flour takes up. The dough should not be hard but definitely not soft either—about the consistency of firm butter. Now weigh the dough, and you can reckon that about half that weight will be the weight of the amount of butter you will need.

After weighing, put the dough in the refrigerator for ten to twelve minutes. Then put it on a very lightly floured board, roll out very quickly into a long strip, and in the middle of this put the butter, which should be firm but not too cold. Fold over the four corners of the strip of dough, so that the butter is covered. Roll out the dough again into a long strip. Don't press, but be always quick and gentle. When the dough is rolled out evenly, fold it in three—one end over the middle, and the other end over the first. Again roll it out, and again fold in three, but this time in the reverse order. Then leave the dough to rest in a very cold place, but not necessarily the refrigerator, for fifteen to eighteen minutes. Then roll out again and fold in three as before, repeat the process in the reverse order and let it rest for another twenty to twenty-five minutes. Again roll out and fold in three, first one way and then the other, so that altogether the dough has been rolled and folded six times since the butter was folded in. This should give you a perfect puff pastry, which can be kept in a damp cloth in the refrigerator and used as required.

When you mix the flour and water at the beginning you can use a little butter if you like—it helps, but it is not essential.

One thing I had to learn in England was the tradition of the wedding cake. In Hungary an elegant wedding had no wedding cake—it was just a reception or dinner, like any other dinner or banquet. All sorts of splendid dishes were eaten, as on any other great occasion, but the nearest to a cake was the sweet we called grilas (see page 186), a very tall affair made of burnt sugar and almonds, highly decorative and excellent to eat. The first time I saw an English wedding cake I could not make out what it was supposed to be.

In Hungary we did not have birthday cakes in the English style, either. Of course on birthdays we had special meals, and then we made the honoured person's favourite gâteau. Sometimes, however, I was asked to make something special for a birthday, and then it might take the form of a cake.

For example, once the wife of a Cabinet Minister told me she was giving a large party on the same day as her husband's birthday, and she asked me if I would think of something amusing and interesting for the sweet. I knew that her husband was passionately fond of polo, so I made a very large chocolate layer cake and, on the top, all in sugar, a proper polo field with players on horseback. It was the most successful birthday cake I ever made in Budapest.

A stranger request was for a cake that would look like cooked goose liver. This was in the nature of a practical joke—a form of humour that does not appeal to me at all, but in our business we cannot set ourselves up as arbiters of our customers' taste. The man who was to receive the cake, in honour of his birthday, was crazy about foie gras. This was his friend's idea of a joke.

*Punch
Gâteau*

We made the cake from a *Punch Gâteau*, which I think is a very good sweet. Men like it with plenty of rum.

For this you simply cut a piece of sponge cake into small cubes, and mix with chopped candied orange peel and glacé cherries and soak this mixture in a mixture of thick sugar syrup and rum. Then sandwich this mixture between two thin layers of sponge in a seven-inch cake tin. Place a heavy weight on top, and allow to stand for twenty-four hours. Take the cake out, glaze with boiled apricot jam, and ice all over with pink fondant (see page 166). Decorate with glacé cherries dipped in granulated sugar.

That is the usual way to make a Punch gâteau. In the case I was talking about, we shaped it like a large goose liver. We covered it with brown marzipan, and put it on a silver dish sitting on yellow marzipan, which resembled goose-liver fat—another delicacy for the Hungarian gourmet. I think it really looked like cooked goose liver, although I could not feel any great pride in it and was glad I did not have to be there when the poor man discovered the joke. He had chosen the wine for it, and ordered fresh melba toast, and was evidently looking forward to a delightful meal. It must have been a very unpleasant shock when he discovered it was a sweet gâteau.

The fact that the birthday cake is traditional in England has given me the chance to have a lot of fun. In 1938 I greeted Neville Chamberlain with a cake for averting the war. In 1945 I celebrated Winston Churchill's part in having won it. My husband planned the cake, which was shaped as a map of England and showed all the places which had been important in the great man's career. London was marked as "10 Downing Street". This was one of a quite famous series as since 1940 the "Churchill birthday cake" had become an annual event. It roused quite a lot of interest, even in a busy place like the Ministry of Food. One cake—again designed by my husband—exhibited all the hats Churchill had worn in the course of his chequered career. It was a huge cake, and achieved world-wide publicity; and the Ministry of Food asked me how I managed to do it with the flour coupons I was allocated. I replied that I could give them three answers, and they should pick the one they preferred:

(1) Members of a grateful nation would have provided all the coupons we needed;

(2) the staff of the bakery offered the necessary coupons to honour the great leader;

(3) no flour coupon whatever was required for that type of cake.

Presumably they accepted my reply, for I never heard any more. I still don't know which of the answers they chose. Perhaps all three.

One of the big events in the social life of Hungary was the celebration of one's name day. This was taken more seriously than a birthday, and we looked forward to our own name days very keenly. A well-known man or woman in any walk of life had to prepare enormous quantities of food and drink for his or her name day, because callers came without invitations and you could never be sure how many would arrive. As I see it now, the preparations were the kind of thing we have for a cocktail party. The drinks varied according to the time of day. In our house my father's name day was an occasion for great celebration, for he was very popular and many people came. I can see it all now—a huge linen basket, lined with a snow-white cloth and packed with pogasha, sweet and savoury, and really big mountains of pastries.

Pogasha is not a cake or pastry but a special Hungarian kind of biscuit, and many varieties of it are made. For savoury pogasha sift two pounds of flour with half an ounce of salt, rub in one and a half pounds of butter, add five eggs, work to a stiff paste, and roll out about half an inch thick. Cut with a small round cutter, brush with egg-yolk, and

Pogasha

place a salted almond on each biscuit. Allow to rest for some time, then bake in a moderate oven. A cheese pogasha can be made by adding cream cheese to the other ingredients, and this can be cut into a different shape.

Linzer Pogasha

The *Linzer Pogasha* is the most famous of the sweet varieties. The ingredients are four egg-yolks, nine ounces of butter, nine ounces of sugar, nine ounces of blanched ground almonds, and nine ounces of flour. Work them all together, add a little salt if the butter is unsalted, a pinch of cinnamon, and a little grated lemon peel. Let the dough rest for an hour in a cool place, then roll it out half an inch thick. Cut out with a small round cutter, brush the top with egg-yolk, and bake till golden-brown.

Another Pogasha

Another kind of Pogasha is made with potatoes as well as flour. Rub through a sieve five ounces of boiled or baked potatoes and blend with five ounces of flour, rub in five ounces of butter, add two egg yolks, a pinch of salt. Roll out, cut and brush as before. Allow to rest for four or five hours, then bake in a moderate oven.

Crackling Pogasha

Then there is *Crackling Pogasha*, one of the best of all. I make my crackling as a by-product, so to speak, of home-made lard. I do not like any bought lard so I make my own. I buy fresh bacon fat—unsalted and unsmoked—and cut it in small pieces and put it in a large saucepan. I add some water, half a tumbler or a full tumbler, according to the amount of bacon; then I cover the pan and boil slowly for about half an hour. Next I put the saucepan on a higher flame, and stir from time to time until the bacon starts to colour. Then I pour off the larger part of the fat and put the pan on a very hot burner. When it starts to sizzle I pour in a few drops of cold milk—keeping out of the way, because it spits!—to make the crackling crack and give it a nice brown colour. Finally I pour off the fat, then put the crackling in a potato presser and press out the fat. In this way I make pure lard and excellent crackling.

A lot of things can be done with crackling. For one, you can eat it on bread with a little salt. This may upset your stomach if you eat too much, but it is worth it. Then you can make a savoury with crackling, and if you want your guests to drink freely you cannot give them anything better. My favourite crackling savoury is Crackling Pogasha, which is where we came in.

You need one whole egg, a pound and a quarter of flour, a pound of minced crackling, half a glass of thick cream, three-quarters of an ounce of yeast dissolved in a little milk, two ounces of butter, and plenty of salt and black pepper. Mix three-quarters of the flour with all the other ingredients except the crackling, and roll out in a soft dough. Mix the remainder of the flour with the crackling, and add two tablespoons of rum. Spread half this mixture on the rolled-out soft dough, fold the two ends to the centre, then the top to the bottom, and leave to rest for half an hour in a cool place. Roll out again, spread the remainder of the crackling mixture over, and fold together in the same way. Let it rest for another half-hour, then roll out again to a thickness of half an inch. Cut with a small cutter, and leave the pieces for another half an hour. Brush over with egg-yolk, and bake in a moderate oven until golden-brown.

One of my favourite sweet biscuits—if you can call it that—is the *Florentine*. Mix in a bowl half a pound of *Florentine* sugar, a quarter of a pound of nibbed almonds, three-quarters of a pound of flaked almonds, six ounces of chopped candied orange peel, two ounces of chopped glacé cherries, one ounce of chopped angelica, half an ounce of ground almonds, half an ounce of flour, and six ounces of fresh cream. Cook gently over the gas. When thoroughly mixed, place in little heaps on greased baking trays, and bake in a moderate oven. When baked, quickly take from the tray, place on wire, and allow to cool. When cool, ice the smooth side of some with chocolate fondant and the other with lemon fondant (see page 166).

Once when I was in America I ate some glorious buns. They were rich, with a lot of nuts, fruit, and burnt sugar. I asked what they were called, and was told they were Danish pastries. When I came home I reproduced what I had seen in America, but I was not satisfied until I could see the original article in Denmark itself. So I decided to go to Copenhagen and learn how to make the real thing.

Some kind Danish business friends in London arranged the trip at my request. They took me quite, quite literally, and organised every minute of it. On the morning after my arrival a young man came to my hotel at half-past ten and said he had been ordered to escort me for the next four days and show me everything worth seeing in Copenhagen.

There were plenty of bakeries to visit, but all were small. The largest, the Royal Warrant Holder, had sixteen assistants and the biggest Konditorei in the city. In the old family businesses, which have been handed down from father to son for generations, there were usually two, or at the most four, workers. Most of them were in very old buildings, so I had to go down to the basement and up to the fourth floor. Of course there were no lifts anywhere. Everywhere I had been announced in advance and was received in the most hospitable way. I had to taste Danish pastries everywhere—the real things, all right, so this was no hardship—but I had to drink a glass of wine everywhere as well. I was kept on the go for four days every day from ten-thirty till six. My guide was the most conscientious young man I have ever known. But he forgot one thing: that I was not so young as he. At the end of those four days I was dead tired.

Danish
Pastries
The dough for *Danish Pastries* is made in the same manner as the puff pastry already described. The ingredients needed are two and a half pounds of flour, six and a quarter ounces of sugar, six and a quarter ounces of margarine, three eggs, one and a half ounces of yeast, and one and a quarter pints of water. When the dough is

mixed, scale off in pieces weighing a pound. After proving for one hour they should be placed on the table and rolled out. Now spread half a pound of butter over the surface of each one-pound piece. Next fold the dough as for puff pastry, give it three turns. To make up the pastries the dough is rolled out thinly, and various shapes and fillings can be used. Typical fillings are cinnamon and chocolate powder, almond paste, sweetened cream cheese, cinnamon and fruit, jam and custard and fruit.

I was lucky enough to be in Stockholm at the time of the famous annual "Festival of the New Light", and I was invited to a factory to see the celebrations. I was fetched by car in the morning before seven o'clock, because the Festival starts while it is still dark. It was held in the factory canteen, which was decorated with stars and candle-lights. The tables were laid for coffee and with pastries of all kinds and shapes—something like German honey cakes. As we began the meal, Swedish girls in long snow-white dresses came in with crowns of candles on their heads, symbolizing the "New Lights". When we had our coffee, several of the factory workers greeted me in Swedish with a toast, and one nice boy had written an English poem in which he welcomed me to Sweden and to the factory.

Afterwards I got the recipes of some of the cakes and biscuits from a Swedish friend. For *Swedish Ginger Cakes*, which I liked very much, you need half a pint of thick cream, a quarter of a pound of brown sugar, half a pound of molasses, a tablespoon of ground ginger, the peels of two lemons, two tablespoons of baking powder, and three and a half pounds of flour. (Again, reduce these quantities proportionately to suit your wishes—and your pocket!) Whip the cream, then add the sugar, molasses, ginger, lemon-peel, and baking powder. Stir well for ten to twelve minutes, then add the flour slowly and work until smooth. Leave the dough in a cool place overnight, then next morning turn it on to a floured board and roll out thinly.

*Swedish
Ginger Cakes*

Cut in any shape you like; if you should happen to have cutters, all the better. Brush with water, and bake on buttered baking sheets in a slow oven.

Butter   Another tasty Swedish biscuit was *Butter Leaves*. For
Leaves   these you need half a pound of unsalted butter, a quarter of a pound of sugar, one egg-yolk, one ounce of ground almonds, three-quarters of a pound of flour, one egg-white, a quarter of a pound of chopped almonds, and four table-spoons of sugar. Mix the butter and sugar until creamy and very fluffy, then add the egg-yolk, almonds, and flour, and mix thoroughly. Put the dough in the refrigerator for two hours, then roll out thinly on a floured board and cut in various shapes, with cutters if you have them. Brush with beaten egg-whites, and sprinkle with chopped almonds and sugar. Put them on a buttered baking sheet, and bake in a moderate oven for about ten minutes. They should be a golden colour.

CHAPTER FIFTEEN

PUDDINGS AND SWEETS

First there is the *Soufflé*, and really it is quite easy to make. Once you have made up your mind that you can and will, failure is impossible.

I use three and a half ounces of sugar, one and a half ounces of flour, one and a half ounces of butter, one-third of a pint of milk, five to six egg-yolks, five stiffly beaten egg-whites and a piece of vanilla pod. First take about one-third of the butter and put in the pan and melt it. Add the flour and mix very well. Warm the milk and gradually add this, then the vanilla pod and the sugar, stirring all the time. When the mixture starts to boil, take it off the fire, remove the vanilla pod, and add the egg-yolks one by one and the remainder of the butter in small pieces, still stirring all the time. Lastly, and very carefully, add the egg-whites, which should have been beaten very stiffly— this is the most important part of making a soufflé—and, very gently but very thoroughly, mix all together. Put the mixture in a china soufflé dish that you have buttered and sprinkled with sugar, filling it only three-quarters full to leave room for rising. Bake in a moderate oven for twenty-three to twenty-five minutes, and serve immediately. The timing is important. The guest has to be waiting for the soufflé, because the soufflé cannot wait.

With slight variations in this recipe, many other soufflés can be made. For chocolate soufflé, for example, you simply add two ounces of melted chocolate to the mixture—but reduce the quantity of sugar a little, as the chocolate is already sweetened. For coffee soufflé you simply add some very strong coffee—and reduce the quantity of milk by the quantity of coffee that you add. Also you will need to add to the sugar to make the soufflé pleasantly sweet.

For orange soufflé, add only grated orange peel to the mixture. Before serving, pour on the soufflé a glass or two of orange curaçao liqueur.

To make a tutti-frutti soufflé, cut all kinds of sugared or candied fruit in small pieces and put them in brandy or rum. Leave to soak overnight, then add to the soufflé mixture. Take care not to put in too much fruit, or it may sink to the bottom.

Strawberry Soufflé

Now here is quite a different sort of recipe, and it is for *Strawberry Soufflé*. Purée half a pound of strawberries. Boil half a pound of sugar in a very little water until a little of the syrup dropped into cold water sets brittle and hard. Add the strawberry purée, and let it boil for a few minutes, stirring all the time; then take it off the fire and let it cool. Beat four egg-whites very stiffly, and mix them with the strawberry purée, then pour the mixture into the soufflé dish. Bake in a moderate oven only for twelve to fifteen minutes.

A similar soufflé can be made with any other fruit.

When I was in the United States I was lucky enough to be invited to one or two American homes. The most exciting of these invitations was to the house of John Rockefeller. I first met the Rockefellers in England, through my great friend the late Seebohm Rowntree. The Rowntrees and Rockefellers were friends of long standing. Then I became friendly with Mrs. Rockefeller's sister, who used to live in Ireland and was married there. So when I was in New York, Mrs. Rockefeller invited me to her home, a penthouse on the top of one of the huge apartment houses owned by the family. Mrs. Rockefeller was young, beautiful, and charming—slim, tall, and most elegant— and her mother was, if anything, even more elegant, beautifully dressed and as dignified as a queen. Of course their home was perfect, but very simple and more English than any English home could ever be. The lunch I had there was also both simple and perfect.

The first course was a fillet of sole poached in dry white wine and served on a very tasty mushroom purée, with a cheese sauce. The meat course a piece of roast veal, long and shiny and golden-brown on the outside but very white inside, and so tender that it melted in one's mouth. It was cooked in butter and a little wine, and served with pear-shaped carrots and tomatoes and creamed sweet potatoes. The sweet was a banana soufflé, and this is the point I have been making for all along.

Purée the flesh of six to eight bananas, and mix with *Banana* a little sugar, a little lemon-juice, three egg-yolks, and a *Soufflé* little cream. Boil together for a few minutes; stir till cool. Whip the three egg-whites with a little sugar, and mix very lightly with the banana purée. Put the mixture in individual china soufflé dishes, and place them in a hot oven for ten to fifteen minutes. When I had this delicious soufflé at the Rockefellers', orange curaçao liqueur was poured on top and it was served with very tiny shortbread petits fours.

A much lesser-known dish, but a favourite of mine, *French* is *French Potato Soufflé*. Bake four or five large potatoes in *Potato* their jackets, take out the insides, and press them through *Soufflé* a sieve. To the sieved potato add three tablespoons of sugar, three egg-yolks, and a pinch of salt. Mix very well together. Whip the egg-whites very stiffly, and add to the mixture very carefully; then pour the whole mixture in a well-buttered soufflé dish. Bake for twenty-five minutes. Dust over the top with icing sugar.

When I make a sweet soufflé I usually serve it with a *Caramel* sauce. Of course different sauces go with different kinds of *Sauce* soufflé, but a good general one is *Caramel Sauce*. It is easy to make. Mix three or four egg-yolks with three or four tablespoons of sugar, add cream or milk, and boil in a double saucepan until it starts to thicken. Meanwhile burn four to five tablespoons of sugar till quite brown—it has to be darker than chocolate—stirring all the time. On to this pour a cupful of milk, and continue stirring until it dissolves completely. Reduce, then add to the sauce. Serve hot.

Wine Sauce
This and other sweet sauces can be used with other dishes besides soufflés. *Wine Sauce*, for example, is excellent with petits fours. Mix three or four egg-yolks with the same number of tablespoons of sugar and a slice of lemon with the peel. Boil in a double saucepan until it starts to thicken. Meanwhile boil up about half a pint of white wine, preferably a dry one, and add this to the sauce, stirring all the time—it must be very, very frothy. Serve hot—immediately.

Rum Sauce
Rum Sauce is just ordinary custard with rum. Make the custard in the usual way, mixing the powder with cream or milk and sugar according to taste. Boil, and when it is thick enough add to it as much rum as you like. When ready add whipped cream. Serve hot or cold.

Raspberry Sauce
Raspberry Sauce also can be served hot or cold. Pass one or two pounds of raspberries through a sieve, add a little sugar and one or two egg-yolks, and boil till it thickens. That's all!

Baked Pineapple
An unusual but very pleasant sweet is *Baked Pineapple*. Peel a large pineapple, and cut nice round slices out of it. Remove the core from each slice. Put the slices close to each other in a buttered fireproof dish, sprinkle with granulated sugar, and put a piece of butter on each slice. Place the dish in a hot oven, basting once or twice with its own juice. When the sugar is brown and melted, pour over a good cupful of thick cream. Mix this with the sugar, and serve hot.

Zabaglione
Zabaglione is a famous Italian sweet, and not difficult to make. Just beat together four egg-yolks and an ounce of caster sugar, and put the mixture in the top of a double saucepan with a quarter of a pint of Madeira or Marsala wine. Stir until thickened—do not allow to boil, or it will curdle. Serve hot or cold.

A great favourite of my childhood was what we called *Malakoff Pudding*. I have no idea where it got its name from, but it was a great treat on special occasions. Begin by mixing together four ounces of butter, five ounces of sugar, five ounces of blanched and ground almonds, and three egg-yolks. When the mixture is really smooth and creamy, add very slowly, drop by drop, a tumbler of milk and two tablespoons of rum. Mix till smooth and creamy again. Take a round dish, preferably glass, and line the bottom of it with sponge fingers; you can, of course, buy them ready made, or, if you prefer it, you can make them at home. Spread some of the creamy mixture on them, then put on another layer of sponge fingers; and repeat until the dish is full. Leave the dish in the refrigerator for a day. Before serving, whip three-quarters of a pint of cream with a little sugar, and cover the whole dish; it is best if you pipe it over with a piping bag. If you like you can decorate the dish with crystallised fruit.

Malakoff Pudding

A popular sweet on the Continent is what is called *English Crème*. It is easy to make and can be given any flavour you like, which makes it extremely useful. Mix three or four egg-yolks with eight to nine ounces of sugar, and beat till very light. Add half a pint of boiling milk, stirring all the time. Let it thicken on the fire, but do not let it boil. When it is thick enough, add a small, very thin sheet of gelatine that you have soaked in cold water; use only the gelatine, not the water as well. Mix in the gelatine, then let the crème get cool; but before it sets, add half a pint of whipped fresh cream. At the same time add any flavouring you like. This can be, for example, vanilla —the pod, not the essence—very strong coffee, melted thick chocolate, raspberry purée, or very finely pounded pistachio nuts.

English Crème

From this crème you can make three or four coloured crèmes. Pour some of the mixture into a mould, which must be very cold and wet, add one of the colours, and let it set; add more of the mixture and another colour, and let this set; and so on, making a rainbow crème. Leave the mould in the refrigerator for three or four hours. Before turning it out from the mould, loosen the sides of the crème with a pointed knife so that it will come away easily.

In the chapter on cakes I spoke of the nearest thing to a wedding cake that we had in Hungary, a sweet called *Grilas*. This is made with sugar and almonds or any other nuts. The nuts must be chopped, not grated. Melt the sugar slowly and work till light brown in colour, then take it off the fire and mix with the chopped nuts. Put it quickly on a greased marble slab if possible—failing that, a board—and roll out with a buttered rolling pin as thinly as possible. Then, while it is still warm, cut it and mould it in any shape or form you like.

Grilas

Once the chairman of a bank told me he had guests coming from Holland, very important business people, and he intended to give a dinner party in their honour. The guest of honour was a tulip-grower—who is not in Holland?—and the banker wanted me to make a suitable sweet for the dinner.

I made a big flower-pot of grilas, and filled it with raspberry, chocolate, and pistachio ice-cream. We covered the top with cocoa powder, and put in a dozen "tulips" in all colours made in sugar and moulded to such perfection that when the butler offered the dish round, the guests first admired it and then smelt it—they could not believe that it wasn't real!

Cold Rice Pudding

Cold Rice Pudding is a very pleasant, refreshing summer dish. Boil half a pound of very well-washed rice, and put in it a small piece of vanilla pod. Boil the rice in milk, but be careful not to overcook it. It is best to measure one cup of rice to two cups of milk, and cook very slowly. When the rice is cooked, let it cool. Then whip up a pint of fresh cream. (If your cream is too thick, add three or four tablespoons of very cold water.) Sweeten with sugar to taste. Cut into small pieces some candied orange peel or crystallised fruit. All the fruit should be sweetened. Take a glass dish, put a layer of rice in the bottom, then a layer of mixed fruit, then a layer of whipped cream; repeat until the dish is full. Decorate the top of the dish with piped cream and assorted fruit. Put the dish in the refrigerator for three or four hours, and serve.

Talking of rice pudding . . . I had an interesting variation on this popular English theme in Tangier. The rice was cooked in milk, but quite dry. It was piled up on the dish like a pyramid, and stripes of powdered cinnamon were sprinkled on it. In an extra bowl soft sugar was served. Mercifully this was one of the few courses at this meal that we did not have to eat with our fingers.

Another pleasant dessert that I had in Tangier was a peach flan made with very short pastry, very thin, which was first covered with hot jam, then had the peaches sliced on to it, and finally was covered with hot jam again. It made a light and very good dessert.

Austrian Noodle (Steier noodle) is another good simple sweet dish, which we used to have mostly for lunch. It was very popular in Hungary, and I think it might be enjoyed by British children and grown-ups too, in spite of the fact that it contains cream cheese, which is not very well known in this country as a sweet. The ingredients are one pound of cream cheese, passed through a sieve, eleven ounces of flour, a pinch of salt, two tablespoons of cream, one whole egg, one egg-yolk, and very little sugar. Mix them together well, and then put the whole dough on a well-floured board and roll it out thin—about the thickness of a matchstick—and cut it in long noodle shapes, each about a quarter of an inch wide. Put it in boiling salted water, and boil for eight to ten minutes. Drain, place in a buttered dish, and put aside. Then take two ounces of butter, and four egg-yolks, and mix well until creamy; add four tablespoons of sugar, the grated peel of one lemon, a few sultanas, and a tumbler of thick cream; mix well, and then mix it all with the noodles. Whip up the whites of the eggs

Austrian (*Steier*) *Noodle*

very stiffly with a little sugar, and mix the whole thing once more. Pour the mixture into a buttered fireproof dish, and bake in a slow oven until golden-brown. Serve hot.

Sweet Ravioli (Two Recipes) In an earlier chapter I gave a recipe for *Ravioli* (see page 142). Two very good sweet dishes can be made with the same dough and in the same way, so that they actually look like ravioli.

For the first you need a stiff plum jam. At home in Hungary we used a special jam made with Zwetschken plums. You can use other jams, but this is the right one because it is exceptionally stiff. We used to make it at home, and we never put any sugar in it because the plums were sweet enough. You can buy these plums here in September and October—they are a very dark mauve colour.

Roll out half the dough very thinly, and place little heaps of jam on it about an inch apart from each other. Roll out the other half, and use it to cover the first one. Press the two sheets of dough together, with the rows of jam between, then cut in squares with a special pastry cutter so that it looks exactly like ravioli. Throw it into boiling water, slightly salted, and boil for ten to fifteen minutes. Take out and put in hot butter, sprinkle with some bread-crumbs that have been browned in butter—be generous with the butter because the crumbs take up a lot—and serve hot.

II The second dish is exactly the same with a filling of cream cheese instead of plum jam. Mix the cream cheese with two or three egg-yolks, and if it is too dry add a little cream. Fill the "ravioli" in just the same way as with the plum jam.

It would be out of place for me to try to tell you how to make a pancake—I know that all of you can make very good pancakes, otherwise there would be no Pancake Day. *Pancake* But I should like to tell you another kind of *Pancake*, a bit different from yours, which I think you might like for a change.

Make a batter with half a pound of flour, three egg-yolks, one ounce of sugar—not more, or it will tend to stick to the pan—a pinch of salt and about a pint of milk. Beat well with the egg-whisk until it is smooth. Beat two egg-whites very stiffly and add to the batter. Mix well. Now butter your pancake pan well—it should be a heavy one—and at the same time put a round china dish in a warm place, ready for use. Then start to cook the pancakes in the usual way. But when each pancake is done on one side, don't turn it or toss it, just slide it on to the warm dish and immediately sprinkle it with a little icing sugar flavoured with vanilla. (A vanilla pod should have been kept in this icing sugar, giving it a pleasant vanilla flavour and aroma.) Go on cooking the pancakes on one side only, sliding them on top of each other and sprinkling with icing sugar, until you have used up all the batter. Then put the dish in a hot oven for a few minutes, and serve hot. Cut it in slices like a cake.

If you like you can layer the pancakes with crushed walnuts or almonds as well as icing sugar.

In an earlier chapter I described how to make a rolled dumpling (see page 145), with a potato dough. With exactly the same dough you can make a *Prune Dumpling*, using Californian prunes. Stone them, and replace each stone with a lump of sugar that has been rolled in cinnamon. Roll out the dough half an inch thick, and cut it into small squares. Put a prune on each square, and shape into nice round balls. Put in salted boiling water, one by one, and boil for ten to twelve minutes—it depends how big the dumplings are. While they are boiling, roast some white breadcrumbs in plenty of butter. Drain the dumplings, roll them in the buttered crumbs, and sprinkle with a little sugar. Serve hot.

Prune Dumpling

CHAPTER SIXTEEN

SANDWICHES AND COLD BUFFET

When I see girls and boys leaving their offices or shops at lunch-time and going into a snack-bar, I feel sad and depressed. Not because a cup of coffee and sandwiches must be a poor meal—on the contrary, if the coffee is good and the sandwiches are well chosen and well made it can be a very pleasant meal indeed. It is ideal for those of us who are in such a hurry to get through life that we cannot afford the time to eat a leisurely lunch. But I am depressed because I know that most of those young people do not expect to enjoy their snack—it does not occur to them to think like that. They simply regard it as something to stop a rebellious stomach from grumbling. I think it is a great shame. Eating should be enjoyed, it should always be a pleasure—we should look forward to all our meals from breakfast to dinner.

One morning, when driving up from my home, I watched some road-repair workers having their tea break and taking out the little bundles their wives had prepared for them. I wondered how often they ate the same things. Then I thought to myself, "If I had to give my husband a little package of food every day, I would make sandwiches with such variety that he would not have the same sort twice for a whole month."

You can make a great variety of cheese sandwiches alone. For example—cream some Roquefort cheese with a little butter or other cheese, spread it on bread, and then cover it with very thin slices of radishes.

Shrimps are not expensive: mix them with a little mayonnaise, and put them between two pieces of buttered bread. Anchovy butter always makes a very pleasant sandwich. You can make a good pâté with pork or veal or chicken liver; for variety, add a few slices of cucumber to this filling. A slice of ham is very refreshing with a few thin slices of apple on it. Any cooked meat, cut in thin slices, is good with cranberry jam or jelly spread on it. Another good filling is egg scrambled with freshly chopped dill or chopped chives. If you want a vegetable sandwich, a little French salad spread on buttered bread makes a good snack. One could go on with ideas for sandwiches for hours.

The word "sandwich" has become international, but there are local variations on the theme. Perhaps the most famous, and certainly one of the most delicious, is the Scandinavian open sandwich, the *smørrebrød*—which means, literally, "buttered bread", and is a single slice of bread, buttered, with something laid on it. Almost any sandwich filling can be used on *smørrebrød*, which is a feature of any cold buffet in Scandinavia.

Nothing is more exciting in Swedish food than the famous *smörgåsbord*, the vast assortment of cold dishes, canapés, and sandwiches that is served in both restaurants and private houses. It is a delight for the eye and the palate.

The first time I saw this fabulous cold buffet I found it quite impossible to count all the dishes, let alone taste them. They were laid out on the huge table in groups. On one part there were half a dozen or so different kinds of cold fish, cooked or tinned—a dish of shrimps, another of anchovies, fish in aspic, smoked salmon, and, of course, various kinds of pickled herring. Another group was of meat—mincemeat balls, cold roast pork, ham, meat in aspic, all kinds of salami and sausages, roast chicken and jellied chicken. Then there were lots of different salads, stuffed hard-boiled eggs, tomato in jelly, a dish of whole mushrooms in a very piquant sauce, a lobster salad very

C.F.L.—O

beautifully arranged, a big dish of lovely red radishes, cucumber salad, and different fruit salads. There was a huge basket with all kinds of bread—black, brown, and white—and biscuits, and there were six to eight kinds of cheese on a large board.

It was all so good that I wanted to taste everything, and my curiosity dragged me from one dish to the next. I tried a good many, but even with the smallest portions it was impossible to get through as many as I would have liked.

Our host was working on a board on which lay some very finely minced raw beefsteak with a raw egg-yolk sitting on top. It looked like a big eye watching us, to see if we appreciated all the food. But it was not able to watch for long, because our host broke it and started to work it in the minced steak. Slowly he worked in the surrounding ingredients—chopped anchovies, chopped capers, onions, chopped chives, black and red pepper, salt and French mustard. He worked with great skill and for quite a time, now and then adding small pieces of butter. When he decided it was ready we were each served with a portion, and it really was a great culinary work of art.

It would be difficult to get the recipes of all the dishes in a Swedish cold buffet, but with a little imagination anyone in any country can put on a good *smörgåsbord*. Here are two recipes that I got from a Swedish friend and used with success.

Meat Balls   The first is for small *Meat Balls*. Mince some beef and the same amount of pork, and add a little white bread soaked in milk or cream, one small onion chopped and sautéd in a little lard for a few minutes, salt and black pepper, just a pinch of sugar, and quite a bit of chopped parsley and chopped chives. Mix all these ingredients together very thoroughly until they are smooth. Taste for seasoning. Shape in very small balls. Put some lard in a frying-pan, and when it is hot put in the balls. Shake the pan all the time they are frying, to keep the balls round. They can be served either hot or cold.

The other *smörgåsbord* recipe is for a *Pâté* made with a   *Pâté*
pound of calf's liver, a quarter of a pound of veal, and half
a pound of fat pork. Cut them in pieces and put them
through a mincing machine. Sauté a chopped onion in fat,
and put this through the machine too, with eight to ten
anchovy fillets. Mix these all together, put through the
machine three or four more times, and then pass through a
sieve. Mix three eggs with one and half cupfuls of cream
and salt and pepper to taste. Beat until well blended, and
gradually add to the meat-and-liver mixture, stirring well
together. Lastly add some diced truffle, and mix again.
Now line a mould with thin slices of fat pork, and fill the
mould three-quarters full with the mixture. Then put the
mould in another tin, which has water in it, and cook it in
this for between two and two and a half hours.

CHAPTER SEVENTEEN

DRINKS, HOT AND COLD

It would be quite absurd and very much out of place if I were to try to tell you how to make a good cup of tea. No, I would never dare do that. I will only say how much I love a cup of tea—and how awful I think a bad cup of tea is.

Tea-making is an art, and I know you have to have feeling to make it. Of course the actual tea that you buy needs to be good, but that is a question of taste. Personally I like and drink Darjeeling, but many of my acquaintances do not agree with me. Still, no one disputes that spending a little more to buy good tea is sound economy, because you need to use much less. The water also is of great importance in tea-making, and perhaps that is one reason why one seldom gets a good cup of tea on the Continent. Another, more obvious reason is that they do not put enough tea in.

I have been told that the teapot ought to be earthenware, and I quite agree. Everyone knows that the pot should be warmed, but I do not think everyone realizes that the inside should be not only hot but quite, quite dry when the tea is put in. Similarly everyone knows that the water must be brought right to the boil, but it does not seem to be so well known that it should only be allowed to boil for a moment.

Even following all the rules does not ensure a perfect cup of tea. There is also the question of the amount of tea you put in—and how long you allow it to draw. I have found that sometimes I make a really good cup of tea—and

194

the next time, using tea from the same packet, water from the same tap, and the same teapot, I make a bad one, or at any rate one not as good as before.

I like China tea very much for a change, but I could not drink it regularly as I do Indian tea. Much greater care needs to be taken in preparing it, as it is undrinkable if too strong and even worse if too weak. Also China tea should, I think, always be drunk from small and delicate cups.

I am not quite sure what the sedative or stimulating qualities of tea in general are, but I recall very clearly that during the war I always put the kettle on when an air-raid warning sounded. A cup of tea is often the answer to a spot of trouble, but according to my experience you must take a spot of trouble in making it.

Then there is Russian tea.

Not long ago I was going round the house to see what junk I had acquired and forgotten about, and I was horrified when I saw what an enormous lot of nonsense I had collected in a comparatively short time. I am not a person who loves shopping—I shop only when I have to, and buy only what I really need—but still the rubbish accumulates. And among the million useless things I found an old family relic—an old family friend, nearly broken to pieces: a samovar.

It came from my husband's home, which was in a valley of the Carpathian mountains. It used to stand on an old table in the office of my husband's grandfather. The same table is now in my husband's office in London, living a much more useful old age than the samovar.

The samovar was, of course, heated by charcoal, and in the old days it was always filled with water and in constant use. On a tray on the table stood six or eight tall glasses, a china bowl containing pieces of sugar cut from a large sugar-loaf, a small plate with some slices of lemon, and a bottle of rum. In the very cold winter days especially, anybody who came to the office—a client or friend, or perhaps the family doctor—would take a glass and help himself.

First he poured in some tea essence from the small cup on top of the samovar—only a little, for the essence was highly concentrated—and then poured on hot water, and added rum or a slice of lemon and lots of sugar. In the Carpathian mountains the winter is very severe, and round my father-in-law's home the snow was yards deep and people travelled mostly on sleighs, wearing big fur-lined coats and fur caps. The room where the samovar was kept was kept warm and cosy by a huge glazed tiled stove, and I am sure the tea made them happy and satisfied.

That is Russian tea. The tea used to come from China. I understand that it was thought it would be ruined if transported by sea, taking on a salt flavour, so it was taken right across Russia on the backs of camels.

In my childhood we lived in the south-eastern part of Hungary, and there also the climate was harsh in winter— dry and sunny, but bitterly cold. When anyone came home from a walk or skating a hot drink was needed, and it was usually punch. For special occasions we had a fancy punch made from tea, sugar, a little lemon, a little white wine, a drop of maraschino, and a little arack. Our everyday punch was made of tea, sugar, rum, grated orange peel, and a slice of orange.

I thought I had seen or at least heard of most ways of serving tea, but I found something quite new to me in an American home. It was in Philadelphia, and I had been invited there for a long week-end. My host and hostess had a lovely villa, with very beautiful English and French furniture and a magnificent collection of old English silver. The service was impeccable in this stately home of America, the two parlour-maids who served at table be-having as if they were made of wax—not a word, not a smile, not a sound to reassure me that they were living human beings.

I arrived just at tea-time, and my host thoughtfully welcomed me with afternoon tea. It was laid in the dining-room on a huge table with beautiful china and lots of other lovely things. There was a great deal of food, including the best Danish ring I have ever tasted—I have tried to copy it since but never really succeeded; I hope because we have not got such a variety of nuts in this country as the Americans have. There were two kinds of tea, Indian and China—but no milk. There was sugar, and there were slices of lemon; but each slice of lemon was stuck with cloves!

When I am a guest I take everything as it comes, but I just could not face tea with lemon and lots of cloves. I therefore said modestly that I always took tea without anything at all, and I expect my taste puzzled my host and hostess as much as theirs puzzled me.

Chocolate is a really heavenly drink if it is made as it should be—and if it isn't, it is better that it should not exist at all. If a cup of chocolate is not something that warms your body and heart, then rather drink a lovely cup of hot water.

In my childhood we drank chocolate only on rare occasions—on birthdays, or as a reward for a very good school report, or at very special parties. Chocolate then was much more expensive than it is now, so in my mind it belonged to the class of luxuries—and, therefore, when we got it we really appreciated it.

We made the drinking chocolate directly from slab chocolate, about a quarter of an hour before it was to be drunk. This slab chocolate was sweetened but not too sweet—a very special, good, hard chocolate. About one ounce per person was used. The chocolate was melted very slowly with a little milk, and stirred all the time. When it was smooth and creamy, the rest of the milk was added. It was heated but never allowed to boil. When ready it was poured into a large china jar kept for the purpose, which had been previously warmed, and then poured into large, specially shaped, very elegant, very thin china cups. Each cup was topped with a spoonful of whipped cream.

With the chocolate was served a beautiful light Kugel-hopf or French brioches or croissants. You cannot have chocolate with anything else. Bread and butter or buttered toast and jam just would not go with it—you have to keep the taste and aroma of the chocolate, therefore you should not mix it with any other food.

Nowadays, of course, making drinking chocolate is made much easier by the use of powdered chocolate prepared specially for this purpose. Yet for sentimental reasons perhaps, or in the belief that it is better, I still make my cup of chocolate from the best existing slab chocolate if I make it at all.

If I make it at all . . . those words, in fact the whole subject, makes me sad and sentimental; because for drink-ing chocolate I feel you ought to have a leisurely life. You ought to have peace in the world and peace in yourself. You ought to be dressed in a worthy gown. You ought to have a few chosen friends in a nice drawing-room, a table laid accordingly, a thin Irish linen table-cloth, and the right, very elegant china.

There is not much for me to say about coffee now. I missed my opportunity—I should have written about coffee-making in this country years ago, when the coffee was really not good, or perhaps even sometimes bad— except, of course, in a very good private house or an exceptional hotel. I remember when we first came to England we were with some English friends in a party when one of them said he did not like coffee. My husband, I think a little rudely, remarked, "How do you know? You have never tasted coffee. What you drink has really nothing to do with coffee."

But it is not so any more. Most private houses make good coffee, nearly all the hotels and restaurants make good coffee, and of course there is good coffee to be had at the hundreds and hundreds of espresso bars. Personally I like the espresso coffee very much—provided, of course, that the quality of the coffee is good, and the quantity used is adequate. I have heard an expert say that the espresso machine just ruins the coffee flavour, but I still like it.

At home, however, I still make it in the old-fashioned, but I think unbeatable, Karlsbader machine. This is a two-piece china machine. You put freshly roasted and ground coffee in the top part, press it down a little, and at intervals pour on it a little water which has reached boiling point but never actually boiled. It is really not a big affair, because whoever makes the coffee can make something else in the meantime, and just from time to time remember to pour a little water in the coffee-pot. The little extra trouble is worth while.

Coffee should, of course, be freshly made every time you drink it. Warmed-up or stale coffee just cannot be coffee. When you make coffee the whole house should be filled with the lovely aroma—the smell of coffee is the one cooking odour that is not offensive outside the kitchen. For white coffee the milk should be hot but never boiling. White or black, I cannot believe that anyone can really enjoy coffee without a little sugar—sugar brings out the flavour of the coffee.

There is a legend that in hot weather a hot drink— especially a cup of tea—will cool you down. I have never believed it, and if I want to be cooled down I have a cold drink like iced tea. It is easy to prepare. Make some very strong tea. Fill a tea-glass with little round ice-balls, or pieces of crushed ice, and pour on it the fresh hot tea.

Iced Tea Coffee and Chocolate

For iced coffee, again, make the coffee stronger than usual. Have your milk very cold, add as much sugar as you like, and mix with the coffee. Keep it in the refrigerator and serve with stiffly whipped cream.

Alternatively, when you have made the coffee—very strong, of course—freeze it in cubes in the refrigerator. Put these into a jug, and serve the cold milk separately, also the sugar and a dish of whipped cream, and just let everybody help themselves.

For iced chocolate I still prefer the slab variety to

powdered chocolate. Melt it slowly, and when it is soft add cold milk; stir, and let it simmer but never boil. It should be thinner than for hot chocolate. When it is cool put it in the refrigerator for one to two hours, and serve with whipped cream.

Strawberry Bowlé   An ideal summer party refreshment is *Strawberry Bowlé*. The evening before the party, sprinkle the strawberries with soft sugar and put them in the refrigerator until the next day. Pour a glass of good French brandy on the strawberries, then a bottle of chilled white wine and finally one or two bottles of chilled champagne.

CHAPTER EIGHTEEN

THE ENGLISH BREAKFAST (HUNGARIAN STYLE)

THE English breakfast is the best and cleverest in the world. It is a real meal, and fortifies you for the whole day. By contrast the Continental breakfast is a very poor affair.

Having said that, perhaps I have no right to say any more. I have only been eating English breakfasts for a little over twenty-five years, so who am I to teach people who have had them all their lives? But I think there is a point there: natives tend to take their national institutions for granted, and it is left to someone like me to point out just how good the English breakfast is. Another point, which I offer more timidly: wonderful as it is, does it really have to be exactly the same every day?

A final point: if you have such a good meal to start the day, surely it is worth while to get up early enough to have it in comfort, and not just bolt it down and then rush off to catch a train or 'bus.

I like to see a man come out of a house in the morning with his hat tilted on one side and a cheerful expression on his face. I like to see him look back with a smile to the door or window, where someone is waving to him, and then set off with a firm brisk tread—but without hurrying—and humming or whistling as he goes. I like to see this, because I am sure he enjoyed his breakfast. That means not only that it was good, but also that he was in time to do it justice.

I am the last person in the world to enthuse about the joys of getting up. I think rising in the morning is distinctly unpleasant, and for me it is the same horror whether it is four o'clock or eleven. I just don't like to leave my bed. So, I think, it would be unreasonable to expect anyone to be down in good time for breakfast but for one thing: another incomparable English institution, the early-morning cup of tea in bed.

When I first came to England I thought it was quite mad to wake you up with "a nice cup of tea". I was staying in an hotel the first time it happened to me, and I could have killed the maid who brought it. Now I cannot get up without it. This early cup warms you, refreshes you, and gives you the courage to get out of your bed. If you have nobody to bring it to your bed, I suggest you make it yourself and take it there yourself—go back to bed, drink the tea and get warm inside, refresh yourself and acquire the energy you need to get over the unpleasantness of getting up.

On the breakfast table I like to see—first of all, of course, some flowers. They are such a cheerful sight. To begin the meal I like grapefruit or another fruit or fruit juice, and then one of your good breakfast cereals or porridge. Why not have a different cereal every day? I have not counted them, but I think there are at least fourteen kinds, including two kinds of porridge.

The porridge I like is Quaker Oats, which I first brown —but only until golden-coloured—with a very little butter: say a teaspoon of butter for two cups of Quaker Oats. Then I boil them with equal parts of milk and water for five to eight minutes, adding a little salt while they are cooking. This porridge should not be sloppy or hard. I have cold milk and golden syrup on the table, and I love this dish. Many friends have told me, with a polite smile, "It is not porridge, but it is very good." Last summer I was assured it was not porridge by someone who ought to know. This was James McBey, the famous Scottish artist, who came and stayed with us for a while. For his first breakfast we gave him some of our porridge, and he was quite upset. He said it was not porridge at all. "If you want to eat porridge," he said,"I will make it for you—but first of all you will have to get the right kind of material. It has to be a very coarse oatmeal." The next morning I had it for him, but he was not satisfied as it was not coarse enough. The next day I bought the coarsest I could get.

We all gathered in the kitchen the following morning. *Porridge* I had a few more guests, and James McBey performed. The water had to be boiling and salted, and then he stood with a wooden spoon in one hand while with the other he let the oatmeal, little by little, drop into the boiling water. He stirred it vigorously for about six to eight minutes. Then everybody went into the breakfast room and was given a plateful of porridge and a cup of cold milk. We had to hold the milk in one hand and the spoon in the other—take a spoonful of porridge with the spoon, dip it in the cold milk, and eat it. In Scotland, James said, you have to eat it standing. I don't see how they manage it, but anyway the Scots are very hardy people.

I don't like porridge cooked this way, but my husband has had it ever since and likes it and believes in it. He says it is very good for him and increases his appetite. James has assured us that if we have this porridge every day we will be very strong and never get a cold all through the winter. He himself looks as if he is made of steel, and is a picture of health with his rosy cheeks and sparkling blue eyes.

After porridge and the other cereals I love your smoked *Fish* *Fish*. I think kippers, boiled or grilled, are very difficult to beat. Smoked haddock, cooked with a little milk in the oven for six to eight minutes, and served with a poached egg—with, of course, a piece of fresh butter melting on the hot fish—is wonderfully tasty and satisfying. I also like roe, fried or grilled on toast. Then I like fresh herrings fried in oatmeal: just ask your fishmonger to clean and bone the herrings, then salt them, put them in a well-beaten egg, then into Quaker Oats; fry, and serve very hot.

Eggs and Bacon

Of course nothing can be better than the most traditional of all the breakfast dishes—*Eggs and Bacon*. I read somewhere that a very serious scientist devoted his life to the study of the mystery of the egg: indeed it is a mystery, but it is also the most helpful and pleasant food, and I cannot imagine what I would do without it. It is important to fry it properly: put it in just as much fat as is necessary. I prefer a little butter. If you put your egg in the frying-pan with a tablespoon of water the yolk will be a little swollen and the egg will be lighter. For this dish it is important to make sure the bacon is a good cut. The thickness is a matter of taste—we like it cut No. 4, which makes a nice crisp bacon. For variety I sometimes buy green bacon, which is less salty and very good.

When they are in season and plentiful we have mushrooms for breakfast. Chop the mushrooms and fry them with a little onion for just five or six minutes. They are good with or without an egg.

Then there are very many kinds of sausages. The good English ones are excellent fried or grilled, and there are also many sorts of Continental smoked sausages that have to be boiled—slowly simmered, not quickly boiled—for ten to twenty minutes according to their thickness.

Hamburger

For still more variety—and I do not think one can ever have too much of that—why not make a nice *Hamburger*? Take half a pound of minced pork, and mix it with a quarter of a pound of stale bread or breadcrumbs, a whole egg, salt, and a little black pepper. Add a little onion which has been fried previously and, if you like, garlic. I think garlic has a wonderful flavour, but of course it must be used with great discretion or it will ruin a dish. When I am making something like hamburger or sausages or mincemeat I use garlic in this way: crush one clove of garlic, put it in warm water, let it soak for ten to fifteen minutes, and then use only the liquid, not the garlic itself. Shape into small flat discs and fry in hot lard.

Another dish we like for breakfast is chicken *Liver* or   *Liver*
calf's liver or pig's liver. This is quickly made, and a very
good dish. Take a large onion, cut it very finely, and fry
in a little lard until it is golden coloured. Add half a teaspoon of paprika, then put in the sliced liver and fry over a
high flame for ten to twelve minutes. Serve with a little
scrambled egg. The salt should be put on only when it is
eaten, otherwise the liver gets hard.

In Hungary we used to eat all sorts of sausages and   *Ham*
salami and *Ham* for breakfast, although we never had
what you call a "cooked" breakfast. I still like to have a
piece of ham in the refrigerator just in case—it always
comes in handy, especially if you live in the country; and
if you cook it yourself it tastes much better than if you buy
it already cooked. I try to buy a corner of raw ham, sometimes smoked, at other times a green ham. I let it soak in
cold water for twenty-four hours. Then I put it in a large
saucepan with fresh cold water, bring to the boil and
immediately change the water for fresh hot water and
repeat this three times.

The last time I add four ounces of brown sugar, or
honey or golden syrup and after it has come to the boil
allow it to simmer till the ham is tender. Instead of the
sugar or honey I sometimes use cider. It should never be
allowed to boil, only simmer. Let the ham cool in the last
liquid.

AU REVOIR

TAKE an inquisitive nature, an eager palate, a feeling of excitement, a hundred and one journeys, a love for cookery, a sheaf of paper and a pen, mix them carefully and there you have my final recipe for the present. Those are the ingredients that have gone into this book.

The hours and weeks I have spent writing it have gone quickly, too quickly, because I could go on for ever. Often I wrote late into the night and indeed had to force myself to stop because all too soon I would be getting up again to start another day of tasting and testing, trying and frying, boiling and perhaps spoiling. In that last thought is, possibly, one of the most important characteristics of the cook—a firm refusal to be discouraged.

I could have gone on writing for a thousand and one Arabian nights, I could have found more and ever more in the almost inexhaustible larder of my memory. I could have written of nice ideas I found in unexpected homes, I could have written of the dishes prepared in some of the grandest and some of the shabbiest restaurants in Europe. I could have written of the times when hungry guests arrived unexpectedly, or of the times when carefully prepared dinners went unaccountably wrong.

That is perhaps at once the thrill and the danger of attempting a book such as this. It is so difficult to stop, and having reached the end the temptation to begin on another is difficult to resist. Never mind, next time it will be better.

However, let me try to sum this one up. The skill you acquire is far more important than the housekeeping budget with which you have to work. A skilful cook can create something quite wonderful even with limited materials, but without skill the most wonderful ingredients will turn to ashes—literally or metaphorically—before your eyes. The most important thing in acquiring skill is enthusiasm—more than that, even, a love for cooking and a joy in cooking. Whatever else you put into your recipe you must put your heart into it, your heart is by far the most important ingredient. It is, of course, much easier to cook for people you love, and so it might be said that people with a friendly disposition are more likely to be good cooks than unfriendly or grumpy people. Chefs are, by reputation, temperamental, but may that not be because it is supremely important to them that the dishes they prepare must be fit to be placed before people they like—even if they have never met them? I like to think so.

Cooking is both a science and an art. In the kitchen you can express your personality and your mood. You can give an expression to your hopes and dreams. You can create, and even though in one sense your creation will be no more than a memory within a few hours of its conception, it is a creation that will never die.

I have no idea how many books have been written about cooks and cooking, but even when I look at my own culinary library, which is extensive but probably incomplete, I am amazed at my cheek in adding to it. I console myself with the thought that it is a library that can never be complete because old ideas and methods are ever giving way to new ones.

Good-bye for now. Perhaps we shall meet again. In the meantime BON APPETIT!

INDEX